# THE
# BEST
## IS YET TO
# COME

**Julius Williams**

ISBN 978-1-68526-269-3 (Paperback)
ISBN 978-1-68526-270-9 (Digital)

Covenant Books
11661 Hwy 707
Murrells Inlet, SC 29576
www.covenantbooks.com

By: *Julius Williams*
9/25/2022

Also by Julius Williams

*Make the Vision Plain*

To my beloved daughter, Tianna. GOD has given you to me as a reward. He has given you to me as a heritage. May you grow up to be what GOD wants you to be, and may you accomplish your dreams.

To my niece, Felecia Blair, who worked very hard for me in the past and also gave some support during my time in prison.

To Dorseta Bucknor, my sister, who has allowed me to stay at her home. May the LORD reward you for your generosity.

And to Elder Rupert Brackett, who has been a good source of strength for me. May the LORD bless you really well.

# CONTENTS

# INTRODUCTION

"Keep hope alive!" was an expression spoken by Jessie Jackson when he was campaigning for president in the eighties. While others gave up, he did not. He never won the nomination, but he continued to the end and supported the nominee.

"The future is there for the taking." This expression of hope is spoken to seniors graduating from schools, colleges, and couples that have decided to get married. You have to learn how to live a happy, fulfilled, and successful life. Things will not always turn out the way you intend but never give up.

Some people go through life having low self-esteem, always thinking negatively. They are focused on their failures, not realizing that they can succeed if they try again, trusting the LORD with all their heart. They all say,

- "I will but not now. Soon I will have a better relationship with GOD, trusting and enjoying His blessings."
- "Soon I will take care of my physical condition."
- "Soon things will be better in my life."
- "Soon I will get caught up with all my work, long enough to make memories for and with my family."
- "Soon I will be making more money. I won't have to worry about how I will pay my bills."

"Soon" unfortunately never comes. We must make good of today. There's nothing we can do about the past. We don't know what the future holds. We can strive to do our best and fully live out our potential.

I know who holds the future, and I know who is holding my hands. I will make mention in this book just how to trust GOD and live your life and improve your situation and your dreams will come through. I can assure you, if you take my advice and read these pages, you will be able to overcome adversities and failures.

Do not lean on your own understanding. Trust the LORD. He will give you enthusiasm, joy, and peace, not for a day, or a week, or a month but for the rest of your life.

In this book, the best is yet to come. You will find the following:

- I Dreamed a Dream
- A Successful Story Is You
- Overcoming Adversities and Trials
- Discover the Power of Your Mind and Words
- Develop a Self-Image That Is Healthy
- Enlarge Your Dream and Vision in GOD
- He Has Blessings That Will Thrust You Years Ahead
- LORD, You Are My Judge
- I Have the Victory, So Can You
- This Is Awesome
- Will You Make the Awesome GOD Your Refuge?
- I Am a Winner
- Get Your Business Straight
- Here He Comes
- Behold I Come Quickly, and My Reward Is with Me
- My Flight to Heaven, the New Jerusalem
- The End

# THE BEST IS YET TO COME

## I Dreamed a Dream

It came to pass that my GOD had given me an overstanding and an understanding in dreams and visions. In the year 1993, I dreamt I was in a big building in College Park, Maryland. After worship, the people moved from one big room to another where I was preparing income taxes. A week later I went to worship in Capital Heights, Maryland, at the New Born Church of GOD, and told the dream to the late Bishop Woodrow Roach. He leaned back in his chair and said to me, "Son, the vision is yet for an appointed time. At the end, it shall speak and not lie. Though it tarry, wait for it. It will surely come. It will not tarry."

Three years went by in which I had joy, sorrow, and sickness. Then in the year 1997, I had another dream. In the dream, the LORD told me to get a computer to do taxes.

I said, "LORD! I don't know how to use the computer, and I can't do the taxes."

He said unto me the second time, "You need to get a computer."

I awoke from my sleep the next morning and told the dream to the one who was sleeping in the bed with me.

She responded, "How are you going to use a computer? How are you going to do taxes? You are peeing blood. You can't sit up for long."

I said to her, "The LORD spoke to me, not you."

She was obviously upset, but I told her the truth. She had a male coworker, Peter, who she said knew about computers. I gave her $850 to give to him to get a computer for me. I got the computer, and the rest is history.

With a few clicks here and a few clicks there, I made it through the computer valley to face the tax mountain that stood in my way. With prayer, fasting, and faith in my GOD, I told the mountain to get out of my way. It did! I did my taxes, and it was pretty fine. One week later, I left my apartment, got into my car, and drove off. About a block down the road, a young man stood by a car with the hood up and looking in the engine. I stopped and ask him if he needed help. He said yes. I reached in the trunk of my car for the jumper cable and gave the car a jump start.

He was happy, very happy, and said, "Thank you, sir." Then he asked me, "What kind of work do you do?"

I said, "I am a tax preparer."

He said to me, "I need to have my taxes done."

He was my first client in my new adventure.

In the summer of 1997, I was admitted to the Adventist Hospital in Takoma Park, Maryland. I had to have a ruptured disc removed from my back. The process is called a laminectomy. It slowed me down but did not stop me from accomplishing my desire. Although the outlook from the doctors were bleak, I had confidence in my GOD, "who healeth all thy diseases" (Psalm 103:3). How precious also are thy thoughts unto me, oh GOD. How great is the sum of them! I kept believing that GOD had my best interest at heart. He would allow me to accomplish my dreams faster than I thought possible. I was winning souls for the LORD. I had to follow my dreams. My wife and I were living in an apartment, paying rent. I just went ahead and packed some boxes for moving. I did not open those boxes until we moved into the new house in February of the year 2000.

I dreamt and had a vision about worshipping and preparing income taxes that was very close to a golf course and the University of Maryland. When we moved into the new house, it was just like in my dream. This was the beginning of an era and an adventure for me. My dream continued full speed ahead. By 2002, I had about 450 clients. People would come to worship for one reason, taxes, but they would not remain. We prayed and asked the LORD to send worshipers. More came for a while. Some had their taxes done and said they would return for worship. Most never did. I never quit. I never gave up. I kept believing there would be better days ahead. I prayed for the people, and they would be healed. Some had their prayers for jobs, houses, cars, and financial blessings answered. I kept my dreams in my mind, and I kept believing things will be better. I kept my head up. My GOD moved, and I baptized several candidates in the name of JESUS CHRIST for the removal of their sins.

I asked the LORD to send me clients, and He did. By year 2006, I had more than eight hundred clients. I would help the people with their rent and their mortgages. I gave loans to people and to some of my clients also. Some loans were large, and some were small. Some did repay their debts; many are still outstanding. I also helped some clients with their credit card bills; others, I helped with their federal and state tax lien. "Be ye therefore merciful as your Father also is merciful" (Luke 6:36).

A good man out of the good treasure of his heart shows that which is good. I was pressed in my heart and in my spirit to do to the people as the LORD was doing to me.

"As we have therefore opportunity, let us do good unto all men, especially unto them who are of the household of faith" (Gal. 6:10).

My GOD showed me that the fear of the LORD is reverence (wisdom) and understanding is to depart from evil. When Solomon was made king, he prayed and asked the LORD for wisdom, knowledge, and understanding; and GOD granted his request. The apostle James said, "If any man lack wisdom, let him ask of GOD, that giveth to all men liberally, without finding fault, and it will be given you" (James 1:5). All the people that cried out to JESUS for help were granted their request. For JESUS said, "And whatsoever ye shall ask in my name, that will I do, that the Father may be glorified in the Son. If you shall ask anything in my name, I will do it" (John 14:13–14).

At Gibeon, the LORD appeared to Solomon during the night in a dream, and GOD said, "Ask for whatever you want Me to give you."

Solomon answered, "You have shown great kindness to your servant, my father David, because he was faithful to You, and righteous and upright in heart. You have continued this great kindness to him and have given him a son to sit on his throne this very day. Now, LORD, my

GOD, You have made Your servant King in place of my father David. I'm only a little child, and do not know how to carry out my duties. Your servant is here among the people You have chosen, a great people, too numerous to count or number. So give your servant a discerning heart to govern your people and to distinguish between right and wrong. For who is able to govern this great people of Yours?"

The LORD was pleased that Solomon had asked for this. So GOD said to him, "Since you have asked for this and not for long life or wealth for yourself, nor have asked for the death of your enemies, but for discernment in administering justice, I will do what you have asked." (1 Kings 3:5–12 NIV)

# DISCOVER THE POWER OF YOUR MIND AND WORDS

# A Successful Story Is You

Over the years one of the most frequent questions the people would ask me is, "How did you manage to be so successful?" My response would always be, "Trust in the LORD, with all your heart, and believe Him." The people who did show up for worship, as soon as it was over, the question was, "How did you become so successful?" I responded as I did before, "Trust in the LORD with all thine heart; and lean not unto thine own understanding. In all thy ways acknowledge Him, and He shall direct thy paths" (Prov. 3:5–6).

> Now after the death of Moses, servant of the LORD it came to pass, that the LORD spake unto Joshua the son of Nun, Moses' minister, saying, "Only be thou strong and very courageous, that thou mayest observe to do according to all the law, which Moses my servant commanded thee: turn not from it to the right hand or to the left, that thou mayest prosper withersoever thou goest. This book of the law shall not depart out of thy mouth, but thou shall meditate therein day and night, that thou mayest observe to do according to all that is written therein: for then thou shall make thy way prosperous, and then thou shall have good success. Have not I commanded thee? Be strong and of a good courage; be not afraid, neither be thou dismayed: for the LORD thy God is with thee withersoever thou goest. (Josh. 1:1–9)

> There shall not any man be able to stand
> before thee all the days of thy life: as I was with
> Moses, so I will be with thee: I will not fail thee,
> nor forsake thee. (Josh. 1:5)

The people were always amazed at the deadly combination of encouragement, prayer, words of wisdom, energy, faith, fear of the Lord, and His presence under one roof. Many of them called it on-the-spot blessings. Not for a moment did I ever thought that I was so brilliant and smart. For, *without* the LORD, my GOD, I am empty, baseless, without understanding or overstanding. Not because I am a dreamer and could interpret dreams! Not because I might have read in a book a few pointers here and there! Not because I had seen experts knowledgeable in tax matters on TV or read their words and work in some newspaper's column. My hope, my trust, and my dreams, and all my knowledge were a special favor from the LORD.

> Who is as the wise man? Who knows
> the interpretation of a thing? A man's wisdom
> maketh his face to shine, and the boldness of his
> face shall be changed. I counsel thee to keep the
> King's commandment, and that in regard of the
> oath of God. (Eccles. 8:1–2)

Most people are quick to brag and boast about what they read in books, achieved in colleges, or of being just born brilliant. Thus saith the LORD,

> Let not the wise man glory in his wisdom,
> neither let the mighty man glory in his might; let
> not the rich man glory in riches: but let him that
> glorieth glory in this, that he understandeth and
> knoweth Me, that I am the LORD which exercise
> loving kindness, judgment, and righteousness,
> in the earth: for in these things I delight. (Jer.
> 9:23–24)

I am always grateful to the LORD for all the little bits and pieces of information that He allowed to come my way. Without the LORD, I can do nothing. Without Him, I would fail. Without the LORD, I would be drifting like a ship without a sail.

If I had all the wisdom of this wide world, if I had all the money that I could buy wisdom, but if I had not the love of my Savior, I would rather be dead than be alive. For it is written,

> I will destroy the wisdom of the wise, and will bring to nothing the understanding of the prudent. Where is the wise? Where is the scribe? Where is the disputer of this world? Hath not GOD made foolish the wisdom of this world? For since in the wisdom of GOD the world through its wisdom did not know Him, it please GOD by the foolishness of preaching, to save them that believe. Jews demand signs and Greeks look for wisdom: but we preach CHRIST crucified, a stumbling block to the Jews and foolishness to Gentiles; but to those whom GOD has called, both Jews and Greeks, CHRIST the power of GOD and the wisdom of GOD. Because the foolishness of GOD is wiser than men; and the weakness of GOD stronger than men. Brothers and sisters, think of what you were when you were called. Not many of you were wise to human standards; not many mighty, not many were of noble birth. But GOD has chosen the foolish things of the world to confound the things that are mighty; and base things of the world, and things that are despised, has GOD chosen, yea, and things that are not, to bring to nought things that are, so that no one may boast himself before Him. (1 Cor. 1:19–29)

Folks were mesmerized by my success and my knowledge of the Word of God. They were amazed about my understanding of the taxes. So each and every time I has an encounter with anyone about my success, I would go back to the dreams that I believe the Lord gave me. There was never a doubt about where and who my success came from. It came not from the east or the west, the north or the south; it came from the Lord. I am talking about an amazing God, a faithful God who makes vessels of honor and dishonor. Of all the degrees that we could ever think of, from kingdom builders to world makers and human creators, none came close to or excel beyond the wisdom and the successfulness of our great God and Savior, Jesus Christ. So I asked myself this question: why was I so successful? I attended Kingston College for one year only. I had no other form of training. But all the words that were in my tongue and in my mouth and all the thoughts in my mind, the Lord knew them all together.

> Bow down thine ears and hear the words of the wise, and apply thine heart unto My knowledge. For it is a pleasant thing if thou keep them within thee; they shall be perfectly fitted in thy lips, that thy trust may be in the Lord; I have made known to thee this day, even to thee. Have not I the Lord written to you excellent things in counsels and knowledge? That I might make thee know the certainty of the words of truth? That you might answer the words of truth to them that send unto thee? (Prov. 22:17–21)

> And the Lord spake unto Moses, saying, "See I have called by name Bezaleel the son of Uri the son of Hur, of the tribe of Judah; and I have filled him with the spirit of God, in wisdom, and understanding, and in knowledge, and in all manner of workmanship, to devise cunning works, to work in gold, and in silver, and in brass, in cutting of stones, to set them in carving of

> timber, to work in all manner of workmanship. And I, behold, I have given with him Aholiab, the son of Ahisamach, of the tribe of Dan: and in the hearts of all that are wise hearted have I put wisdom, that they make all that I have commanded thee. (Exod. 31:1–6)

My GOD is a success story. I thank Him for my mind. Without GOD, I could do nothing. But with GOD who strengthens me, I can do all things through Him. Many lives have been changed with the LORD working in me.

The telephone rang! I picked up the receiver.

"Tax service, may I help you?"

"Is this Mr. Williams?" the voice stated. "You were highly recommended by several of your clients. They said you are the best."

This is just one of the many calls me or my helpers have received from people who were impressed by what they had heard. The devil did not like me for this and sought to slay me. On many occasions, he tried to kill me.

> "The thief cometh not, but to steal, and to kill, and to destroy," said JESUS. "I am come that they might have life, and have it more abundantly." (John 10:10)

Strong, bold, and determined, I pressed ahead, knowing for sure that JESUS CHRIST, the LORD and my GOD, was always with me. I would increase more and more.

> Blessed is the man that thrust in the LORD, and whose hope the LORD is. For he shall be as a tree planted by the waters, and spreads out her roots by the river, and shall not see when heat cometh, but her leaves shall be green, and shall not be careful in the year of drought, neither shall cease from yielding fruit. (Jer. 17:7–8)

My clients would say to me, "You are truly blessed of the LORD. We know you are a man of GOD, and the LORD is with you. From the moment we pulled up to park, we could feel the presence of the LORD. While coming down the steps into the waiting area, we felt GOD's presence."

They would say, "Go ahead, do your work, and just put those numbers in the computer. We trust you."

The devil did not like it. He would come at me from every angle, time after time, to hinder me. I would always bow my head, fall on my knees, lie down flat before the LORD. I asked Him for guidance, for direction, for protection in the way I should go. The LORD was always with me. His words were my comfort. His word is still my comfort. "Comfort ye, comfort ye, My people," says Your GOD.

> And the LORD appeared unto Isaac, and said, "Go not down into Egypt, dwell in the land which I shall tell thee of: Sojourn in the land, and I will be with thee, and will bless thee; for unto thee, and thy seed, I will give all these countries, and I will perform the oath which I sware unto Abraham thy father. And I will make thy seed to multiply as the stars of heaven, and will give unto thy seed all these countries, and in thy seed shall all the nations of the earth be blessed. (Gen. 26:2–4)

> Then Isaac sowed in the land, and received in the same year an hundred-fold" And the LORD blessed him. The man Isaac wax great went forward, and grew until he became very great. he had possession of flocks, and possession of herds, and great store of servants. And the Philistines envied him. For all the wells which his father's servants had dug in the days of Abraham his father, the Philistines had stopped them, and

filled them with earth. And Abimelech said unto Isaac, "Go from us, for thou art much mightier than we. And Isaac departed thence, and pitched his tent in the valley of Gerar, and dwell there. And Isaac dug again the wells of water, which they had dug in the days of Abraham his father, for the Philistines had stopped them after the death of Abraham: and he called their names after the names by which his father had called them.

And Isaac's servants dug in the valley, and found there a well of springing water, and the herdmen of Gerar did strive with Isaac's herdmen, saying, "The water is ours." He called the name of the well Esek, because they strove, and quarrel with him. And they dug another well, and the men of Gerar quarrel and argued for that also, and he called the name Sitnah. And he removed from there, and dug another well, and for that one they did not quarrel, and he called the name of it Rehoboth; and he said, "For now the LORD has made room for us, and we shall be fruitful in the land." (Gen. 26:12–22)

With success comes opposition! With success comes threats! With success comes examinations! With success comes malice and persecutions! But the LORD is always standing by my side. The LORD is the strength of my life. I have always, always made the LORD my guide in my walking, in my talking, in my singing, and in my praying.

And it shall come to pass, if thou shall harken diligently unto the voice of the LORD thy GOD, to observe and to do all His commandments that I command thee this day, that the LORD thy GOD will set thee on high above all nations of the earth. And all these blessings shall come on thee, and overtake thee, if thou shall hearken unto the voice of the LORD thy GOD. Bless shall thou be in the city, and bless shall thou be in the field. Blessed shall be the fruit of thy body, and the fruit of thy ground, and the fruit of thy cattle, the increase of thy cows, and the flock of thy sheep. Blessed shall thou be when you come in and blessed shall thou be when you go out. The LORD shall cause thine enemies that rise up against thee to be smitten before thy face: they shall come out against thee one way, and flee before thee seven ways. The Lord shall command the blessing upon thee in thy storehouses, and in all that thou settest thine hand unto; He shall bless thee in the land which He the LORD thy GOD gives thee. The LORD shall establish thee an holy people unto Himself, as He has sworn unto thee, if thou shall keep the commandments of the LORD thy GOD and walk in His ways. And all the people of the earth shall see that thou art called by the name of the LORD, and they shall be afraid of thee.

The LORD shall make thee plenteous in goods and in the fruit of thy body, and in the fruit of thy cattle, and in the fruit of thy ground, and in the land which the LORD sware unto thy fathers to give thee. The LORD shall open to thee His good treasure, the heaven to give thee rain unto thy land in his season, and to bless all the work of thy hand, and thou shall not borrow. The LORD shall make thee the head, and not the tail; and thou shall be above only, and you shall not be beneath if you hearken unto the commandments of the LORD thy GOD, which I command thee this day to observe and do them. (Deut. 28:1–13)

The Lord, my God, has made me a promise, for me to prosper and have good success. So the just shall live by His faith.

When you make promises to your children, they are looking for you to come through with what you have promised. Some years ago, the story told of a father who really wanted his son to do well and excel in his exams. So he said to his son, "Son, if you study hard and pass all ten subjects, I promised you I will buy you a car."

He was very excited and said to his father, "Daddy, would you really buy me a car?"

The father said, "Yes, son, I will."

The young man went out and immediately reach for his books. He dived into them without mercy. He did not play around as most of his friend did. He sat the exam with confidence. Long last the results were published. With enthusiasm, he ran and fetched the gazette. When he opened it, his name was the first listed. He had passed all ten. He went to his father and said, "Daddy, I passed all ten of my subjects. Can I get that car that you promised me." He kept on asking his father until he was tired of him reminding him of his promise. He went and bought him a new Fiat and appeased himself.

## Overcoming Adversities and Trials

There were many adversities along the way. There were some people I wish I had never met. Some were outright disrespectful and feisty. On some clients, you could just see trouble! You just had that feeling that something was about to go wrong. Here I am, trying to clear up your taxes that someone else had messed up, and after I did, there was trouble. Some folks would just walk in possessed with evil spirits, and you could feel them and see them. I kindly asked them to leave in Jesus's name. They would always come back to see me.

I was threatened by members of my own family. Two women lied on me to the Internal Revenue Service. I was threatened by some clients who just wanted to have their own way. I told them whatever their hearts desire, whatever your mind tell you to do, do it. What I am doing, if it be of God, you nor the authorities cannot overthrow it. I would always interject the Word of God in everything I say and do, knowing that life is filled with adversities, disappointments, and setbacks. I constantly had my trust in the Lord. I have come to the realization that it makes no difference what you set your heart and mind to work on, you are prone to make mistakes, which can be corrected. We wouldn't be humans if we don't make an error. On many occasions, I had to talk to myself: "JW, stop from being so hard on yourself." In all my life, my deepest fear was what people would say about me.

I made many mistakes and corrected them. When an error or mistake is corrected, the problem is fixed or solved, never existed. If there was never a problem, I wouldn't know how to solve them. Here I am, at the right place, answering questions and having the problems solved. The God that I serve is a problem solver. And whatsoever you do, do it heartily as the Lord and not unto men. (Col. 3:23). My client knew very well that with me helping them, their problems were solved. It was not in vain. But even after what I had suffered before and was shamefully treated, I was bold and more determined to stand on the Word of GOD, speaking to the people the gospel of JESUS CHRIST and doing their taxes with much contention. It was never in me to give up easily. A winner never gives up. He who gives up never wins. I also made some bad investments along the way because I did not seek GOD for direction. But through it all, I learned to trust in JESUS. I learned to trust in GOD, who has kept me through all my gains and losses.

"To everything there is a season, and a time to every purpose under the heaven: A time to get and a time to lose; a time to keep, and a time to cast away" (Eccles. 3:1, 6). Throughout life, whether winning or losing, I truly believe I should concentrate on the problem solver, not the problem. As a winner, you will always have folks coming around. No one really wants to deal with a loser.

By the year 2011, my clientele increased to more than 1,400. The LORD just keeps on doing great things for me. I had a full-time secretary and two part-timers to help with the workload. The sky is the limit for what I can have. More clients! More money! More problems to solve! I kept thanking the LORD for His blessing on me. I am preaching the gospel! I am praying for the people! My bills are all paid. What more could I ask? I had a plan. The LORD has a plan. The enemy always have plan. His plan is to kill, steal, and destroy. But I will not be deterred. Greater is He that is in me than he that is in the world. I was motivated by the power of my GOD, sharpening the countenance of my clients and friends. As iron sharpens iron, so one person sharpens the countenance of his friend (Prov. 27:17).

From about February 2005, H & R Block was sending me information, asking to purchase my business. At no time did I ever discuss or made mention of selling my business. This was what H & R Block kept doing every three or four months, all year, until 2011. I knew something was suspicious about their letters and their offer.

On October 24, 2011, at about 10:25 a.m., my wife called me from the top of the stairs, saying, "Dad! Some people are here at the door for you." So I came up the steps, opened the door, and went outside to greet them. They were federal agents, five men and six women, one of whom was Rod Rosenstein, US Attorney for the

District of Maryland. They wanted me to sign some fake documents. We were in the basement that I used for worship. I prayed over the documents. The Spirit prompted me not to sign. They went about looking for money. They found none. They took all my documents and my clients' tax records. They interrogated my wife for about six hours. They finally went away at 5:15 p.m., and I never heard from them until October 2013. A few days after that incident, I went and consulted a lawyer. I told him what transpired. He charged me $20,000, with a down payment of $5,000.

August of 2013, the lawyer informed me that Rosenstein informed him of one charge against me. He was asking for me to enter into a plea agreement. But the lawyer said, "We will not accept the plea." On October 24, 2013, they came to me again. This time they took me before Judge Day. They asked the judge to put a bond on me. He refused! The one charge they had was filing false tax returns. The judge's order for me was, "When you prepare any new return, give copies to your lawyer within five days and surrender your passport." The next day after I saw the judge, probation officer Troy Scott from the court in Green Belt, Maryland, paid me a visit. I told him I had just amended two tax returns. He said, "That is okay! Give them to your lawyer." I called the lawyer. Someone answered and said, "He is not in office. He is out of town. He will be back on Tuesday. Leave him a message on his machine." I did! Later, I called the lawyer and told him of the returns. He said, "I will inform the judge." He did not.

On Monday, November 11, this lawyer called me. "We have to go before the judge 2:00 p.m. on Tuesday," he said. We went before the judge, and he asked, "Why did your client not follow my order?" He blatantly lied to the judge and said, "Mr. Williams misunderstood the order, Judge." The judge was very upset with me. The lawyer didn't inform the judge that I gave him the information, but he did not give it to the judge within the five-day timeline. Remember the man from the court that stop by my office? He gave the judge the date when I prepared those returns. The judge made a new order.

"Updating the previous order for 2014 tax year, all the returns that you prepare must be brought to the United States Attorney's

Office, within five days, every week. Did you hear the order, Mr. Williams?"

"Yes, Your Honor," I replied.

I completed 940 tax returns, all had to be mailed, both state and federal, plus copies for the clients. Having obtained help from GOD, I made it through and continue until this day. It was a lot of work, but GOD kept me, and I did not give up.

On my second visit before the judge, my adversaries increased the charges to six. By January 2014, the charges went up to twenty-eight. The enemy turned up the pressure on me, trying to convince me that I was at the point of no return. The lawyer took me to his office.

"Your charges are up to twenty-eight, I have to charge you $10,000 more," he said. He reached into a folder, pull out an agreement and slide it across the desk to me.

When I look at the document, the $20,000 we originally agreed on was now up to $30,000. The amount was changed with the wording thereof, but my original signature was still there. I shook my head, obviously still distraught by the mere thought of it.

"This is not the agreement that I signed," I said to him.

"Take it or find yourself another lawyer," he said to me.

I got up and said to him, "Have yourself a bless day, sir."

On February 17, 2014, I was in my office with my client and three more in the waiting area. Felecia, my assistant, knocked on the door.

"Come in!" I said.

"Your attorney is on the line," she said.

"Tell him I am with a client. I will call him as soon as I am through," I said to her.

When I was through with the client I returned the call.

"Attorneys' office," the young lady said.

"May I speak to Mr. Fatai?" I said.

"He is not in the office," she said.

"Tell him, Mr. Williams called."

The next day he called back.

"This is Mr. Williams," I said.

"Mr. Williams, you are avoiding my calls. If you will not comply with the retainer agreement to represent you as your attorney, I will file a motion to withdraw as your attorney," he said.

I said to him, "Go ahead and do as you please, sir."

He went and did what he said he would do.

## The Witness of a Good Profession

On March 14, 2014, I went to court to represent myself. They had a public defender, Ms. Whalen, waiting for me. She came to me and introduced herself. I told her I already have counsel, but I will use her as a backup.

She asked me, "Where is he?"

I said, "He is here with me. You just can't see Him, and He never loses a case."

Looking at me with a smile on her face, she said, "Okay."

We went into the courtroom, and the court was called to order.

Ms. Whalen said, "Your Honor, I am here to represent Mr. Williams, but he already has counsel. I will stay as a backup."

Judge Grimm said, "Mr. Williams, did you study the bar? What school did you attend? Did you go to college?"

I replied, "Your Honor, I did not study the bar. I completed high school. I went to Kingston College for one year, sir."

He said, "Do you know the consequences you will have if you represent yourself?"

I said, "Your Honor, let me tell you about my Counsel. He is wonderful counselor, the mighty GOD, He is the Everlasting Father and the Prince of Peace. He is with me in this courtroom."

He said to me, "Mr. Williams, faith does not work in the courtroom."

I said, "Your Honor, you might have thought it was your own wisdom and your knowledge that put you on the bench. The LORD JESUS CHRIST did, even for you to tell me what you will."

He said to me again, "I just told you faith does not work in the courtroom."

I said, "Your Honor, sorry to interrupt you, sir, but Hebrews 11:1–2 says, 'Now faith is the substance of things hoped for. The evidence of things, not seen. By faith the elders obtained a good report.' By the way, Your Honor, let me tell you what my Counsel is telling me in my ears to tell you, sir. That if you, your four court reporters, the two prosecutors to my right, and the attorney to my left will humble yourselves, I, Julius Williams, GOD's anointed servant and the tax preparer from 8704 Thirty-sixth Avenue in College Park, Maryland, will baptize you in water in the name of JESUS CHRIST for the removal of your sins, and you shall receive the Holy Spirit that GOD promised to you and your children, as many are far off, as many as the LORD our GOD will call. Your Honor, save yourself from this homosexual and lesbian generation."

The Spirit of GOD moved in me, and I spoke in tongues for a while.

Then I said, "Your Honor, sir, I hand over to you."

The judge pushed his glasses up on his face and tilted forward in his chair and said, "Mr. Williams, I've told you, faith does not work in the courtroom."

After this engagement between us, the meeting was adjourned.

## Lying Witnesses

I was again ordered to appear before Judge Day on May 9, 2014. The prosecutors put on the witness stand an officer who I had never met before. This debacle between the prosecutor and the witness was a failure. The judge did not believe them. He asked for them to produce two or more witnesses. After their consultation, they asked the judge for six months to produce those witnesses. He said no and gave them four business days to do so.

The next meeting before Judge Day was Friday, May 16, at 1:00 p.m. When we reached the courthouse, my niece, Felecia, said to me, "Mr. Williams, look! Your clients from Virginia." These were my clients. I have prepared their taxes for the past seven years. They were husband and wife who were always verbally fighting in my office over tax money. To pacify the situation, they asked me to pray for them as we held hands. I had previously told them what the Feds were doing to me. On seeing them, I approached with my arms wide open. They looked at me like when gazelles see a lion on the prowl and immediately turned away. After this encounter, I turned around. To my surprise, I came face-to-face with two more of my clients. I had prepared their taxes for the past four years. I greeted them, but they did not respond.

Of the four witnesses, two of them were called to the witness stand. They blatantly lied to the judge. At the end of their testimony, the judge said, "I hate to do this! I hate to do this! Marshals, he is in your hands."

The marshals took me and carried me to a location in Southern Maryland. When the vehicle came to a complete stop, the officers came to the back of the vehicle and opened the door. On my way out, I said, "Oh my GOD, this is what I saw in the dream."

One of the officers said to me, "What are you talking about?"

I said, "Sir, this is the same building with the horseshoe on the front that I saw back in 2012 where I was locked up. I asked the LORD in the dream, 'Why am I locked up?' But I didn't get an answer."

The officer responded, "Hot be damned."

I was held at this location for eight months without trial.

The treatment was very horrible. One day two men were playing chess. They were eating chips and cheese out of the same dish. Suddenly, they started cursing and fighting each other. They were both bleeding badly. Suddenly, the siren went off. "Lockdown, lockdown," were the words echoing over the speakers in the roof of the building. About twelve officers came.

"Down on the ground, down on the ground, every one of you."

I was in a little passage on the steps and was slow to get down because of the injury to my back (on which the doctors did a laminectomy). Two officers came and grabbed me, threw me down, twisted my back. I was sweating profusely and in severe pain. Two officers rushed me to the doctor in the building, Charles County Detention Center. After they took my blood pressure, they found it was so high. They immediately rushed me to the hospital. On examination, the doctor said, "How is he still alive? This man should be dead."

I was kept there for two days for observation and then released into the custody of the officers. I am still here. Bless the LORD.

## The Sentencing

On January 5, 2015, I was brought before Judge Grimm for sentencing.

After about ten minutes in court, I heard the words, "All rise, the Hon. Paul W. Grimm presiding. You may be seated."

Then said the judge, "We are gathered here today for the sentencing of Julius Williams. Is he in the building?"

My cocounsel responded, "Mr. Williams is present, Your Honor."

After the judge addressed the gathering, he asked counsel to respond.

Ms. Whalen said, "Your Honor, you should let Mr. Williams go. I think you are making a big mistake locking him up."

The judge said, "I don't make mistake. I am doing what Congress said." Then he continued, "Because of the plea agreement, the defendant is adjudged guilty of the offences—fraud and false statements, fraud by wire, radio or television fraud, identity theft. The sentence is imposed pursuant to the Sentencing Reform Act of 1984 as modified by US v. Booker. 125 S. Ct. 738 (2005). *It is further ordered* that the defendant shall notify the United States Attorney for this district within thirty days of any change of name, residence, or mailing address until all fines, restitution cost, and special assessment imposed by this judgment are fully paid."

## Counsel's Address to the Court

"Your Honor, may I address the court?"

The judge responded, "You may."

Counsel said, "Judge, I do believe you are making a big mistake in the amount of sentence you are giving Mr. Williams. You have heard and seen the demonstration of his religiosity. You have two Spanish gentlemen over whom you presided in this very courtroom.

They did more than what Mr. Williams is accused of and you gave them less time. Their restitution is far less than what you are asking Mr. Williams to repay. I think you are doing a great injustice to Mr. Williams."

Judge Grimm said, "I don't make mistake. I am doing what Congress said. Would anyone like to speak on Mr. Williams's behalf?"

Bishop Mair, who I had worshiped with in the past, spoke good on my behalf. Some family members also spoke good on my behalf. The judge read a few letters that were well written to show support for me.

Judge Grimm said, "Counsel, does your client have anything to say?"

She said, "Yes, Your Honor. Mr. Williams would like to say something."

## Overcoming Adversities and Trials II

## My Defense

I said, "To the Honorable Judge, grace and peace be multiplied to you and your staff. I have been brought before the judges for charges against me for my behavior and the judgment that I made for my clients. Do you not know, Your Honor, that the saints shall judge the world? And if the world will be judged by me, am I unworthy to judge the smallest matters? Your Honor, the saints shall judge the angels. How much more things that pertain to this life? I accept the wrong and let myself be cheated, trying to save others. The LORD told me in His Word to honor all people. To submit myself to every ordinance of man for His, CHRIST's sake. Whether to kings, presidents, or governors, and magistrates, and those who are sent by them, for the punishment of evildoers and for praise of those who do good.

"For this is the will of GOD. That by doing good, I may put to silence the ignorance of foolish men as free, yet not using my liberty as a cloak for vice, but as a bond servant of GOD." (1 Pet. 2:15–16). For to this purpose I was called to be a preacher and a tax preparer to help the people. JESUS CHRIST also suffered for us, leaving us an example, that we should follow His steps. JESUS committed no sin, nor was deceit found in His mouth, who when He was reviled, did not revile in return. When He suffered, He did not threaten but committed Himself to the Spirit who judges righteously. Jesus bore our sins in His own body on the cross, that we having died to sin might live for righteousness by whose stripes I am healed.

"The eyes of the LORD are on the righteous, and His ears are open to their prayers, but the face of the LORD is against those who do evil." And who are they that will harm me if I become a follower of what is good? But even if I suffer for what I did, I am blessed. I am not afraid of any threats, nor am I troubled. But I sanctify the LORD GOD in my heart and always ready to give a reason for the things I do and for the hope that is in me, with meekness and fear. Having a good conscience that when they defame me as an evildoer, those who revile my good conduct in judgment may be ashamed. You are prosecuting me. *You* are prosecuting the LORD JESUS CHRIST. It is hard to fight against GOD. For this purpose my actions, Your Honor, I am before you again so all may hear.

"You are inexcusable, whoever you are who judge, for in whatever you judge another you condemn yourselves. For you who judges practice the same things." Those who have accused me received orders from those who are persecuting me, went as far as overseas. They beguile and tricked people who gave false statements, and some they granted immunity for their statements and actions. Do you all believe you will escape the judgment of GOD? Who will render to each one according to his deeds, who continuing to do good, seek for glory, honor, and immortality. But to those who are self-seeking and do not obey the truth but obey unrighteousness, it will be indignation and wrath, tribulation, and anguish on every soul of man who does evil, of the Jews, Greeks, and Gentiles. But glory, honor, and peace to everyone who works what is good."

"There is no partiality with GOD. For as many as have sinned without law will also perish without law. And as many as have sinned in the law will be judge by the law. For it's not the hearers of the law are just in the sight of GOD, but the doers will be justified. For when African Americans who do not have the law, by nature do the things that are in the law. We, although not having the law, are a law to ourselves. Who show the work of the law written in our hearts, our conscience also bearing us witness. And between ourselves, our thoughts accusing us or else excusing us. In the day when the LORD GOD will judge the secrets of men by JESUS CHRIST, according to my gospel."

"You who have studied the law and claims you know the law and know GOD's will and approve the things that are excellent, being instructed out of the law, and are confident that you yourselves are a guide to the blind and a light to those who are in darkness. You are an instructor of the foolish, a teacher of babes, having the form of knowledge and truth in the law. You, therefore, who teach another, do you not teach yourselves?" Your Honor, sir, the unrighteous will not inherit the kingdom of GOD. Neither fornicators, idolaters, adulterers, homosexuals, lesbians, thieves, covetous men and women, unclean lips, drunkards, revilers, nor extortioners will inherit the kingdom of GOD. And such were and such are some of us. But I am washed. I am sanctified. I am justified and made clean in the name of the LORD JESUS CHRIST and the Spirit of our GOD. All things are lawful for me, but all things are not expedient or helpful. All things are lawful for me, but I will not be brought under the power of any.

Your Honor, sir, the eyes of the LORD are upon the righteous and whose ears are open wide to all their calls. But the face of the LORD is against those who do evil. The LORD is good to me. Who forgives all my sins and my iniquities, who heals all my diseases, who redeem my life from destruction, who crowns me with loving-kindness and tender mercies, who satisfied my mouth with good things. The LORD is merciful and gracious, slow to anger, and abounding in mercy. The LORD will not always strive with us, nor will He keep His anger forever. The LORD has not dealt with us according to our iniquities. He is slow to anger and abounding in mercy, for He knows our frame. He remembers that we are dust. Our days are like grass, as the flowers of the field, so we flourish. Then His wind passed over us, and we are gone and take nothing with us.

"As far as the heavens are high above the earth, so great in His mercy toward those who fear Him." As far as the east is from the west, so far has the LORD removed our transgressions from us. As a father pities his children, so the LORD pities those who fear Him. The LORD look down from the height of His sanctuary. From heaven, the LORD views the earth and hear the groaning of this prisoner and appointed me to be prosecuted, sentenced, and, after that, have the charges dismiss.

"Your Honor, sir, those who will live godly will suffer prosecution. Who will bring a charge against GOD's elect? It is GOD who justifies. Who is he who condemns? It is CHRIST who dies and, furthermore, is also risen. Who is even at the right hand of power, who also makes intercession for us. Who shall separate me from the love of JESUS CHRIST, my GOD? Shall tribulation, distress, or persecution, famine, or nakedness, peril, or sword? As it is written, 'For thy sake, O GOD, we are killed all the day long. We are counted as sheep for the slaughter.' Yet in all these things I am more than a conqueror through Him who loves me."

At this point the attorney spoke softly in my right ear. "You are making the judge really, really upset."

## My Defense Continues

I continued, "For I am persuaded that neither death, nor life, nor angels, nor principalities, powers, nor things present, nor things to come, height, dept, nor any other created thing, shall be able to separate me from the love of GOD, which is in CHRIST JESUS, our LORD. What shall we say to these things? If GOD is for me, who can be against me (Rom. 8:31–39)?

At this point, the judge interjected. "How much longer, Mr. Williams?"

"Just a few more words, Your Honor," I said. Then I continued, "Thus saith the LORD, 'Let not the wise man glory in his wisdom, let not the mighty man glory in his might, nor let the rich man glory in his riches. But let him who glories glory in this, that he understand and knows Me, that I am the LORD, exercising loving-kindness, judgment, and righteousness in the earth, for in these I delight.'

"I am not ashamed of the gospel of JESUS CHRIST, for it is the power of GOD to salvation, for everyone who believes (Rom. 1:16). Judge, men and women of this court, prosecutors, attorneys, and audience, the kingdom of heaven is at hand. Repent and be baptized in water, in the name of JESUS CHRIST for the removal of your sins. You shall receive the gift of the Holy Ghost. For it is promised to you and your children and to all who are far off, as many as the LORD our GOD shall call. Be saved from this wicked and perverse generation. Whoever accepts the call of GOD, I will baptize you in the name of JESUS CHRIST. Peace be unto you all (Acts 2:37–39)."

# Judgment Time

The judge said, "After hearing everything that has been said, this court has made its decision. The defendant is hereby committed to the custody of the United States Bureau of Prisons to be imprisoned for a total term of sixty months, consisting of thirty-six months as to count 14, thirty-six months as to count 18. Thirty-six months as to count 20 of the indictment, all to run concurrent. And twenty-four months consecutive as to count 27 of the indictment. The defendant shall receive credit for time served from May 16, 2014 as to counts 14, 18 and 20 of the indictment. The defendant is remanded to the custody of the United States Marshal."

## Supervised release conditions

"Upon release from imprisonment, the defendant shall be on supervised release for a term of one year as to count 14, one year as to count 18, one year as to count 27, and three years as to count 20, all to run concurrent.

"The defendant shall report to probation office in the district to which the defendant is released within seventy-two hours of release from the custody of the Bureau of Prisons."

## Access to financial information

"The defendant shall provide the probation officer with access to any requested financial information."

## Credit restriction

"The defendant shall not incur new credit charges or open additional lines of credit without approval of the probation officer."

## Internal Revenue Service

"The defendant shall cooperate with the Internal Revenue Service in the determination of the civil tax liability and the payment of any Taxes, Penalties, and Interest that are due."

## Restitution

"The defendant shall pay restriction in the amount of $1,000,000,00. Restitution shall be paid both through the Inmate Financial Responsibility Program and in monthly installments of $100.00, to commence thirty days after the defendant's release from incarceration."

## Special assessment

"The defendant shall pay a Special Assessment in the amount of $400.00, which is due immediately.

"The defendant must make restitution (including community restitution) to the following payees in the amount listed below.

"If the defendant makes a partial payment, each payee shall receive an approximately proportioned payment, unless specified otherwise in the priority order or percentage payment column below:

Name of Payee:

Clerk, U.S. District Court
6500 Cherrywood LN
Greenbelt, MD 20770

Restitution Order:

$1,000,000.00

"The court determined that the defendant does not have the ability to pay interest and it is ordered that: the interest requirement is waived for the restitution.

"Upon a finding of a violation of probation of supervised released, I understand that the court may (1) revoke supervision, (2) extend the term of supervision, and/or (3) modify the conditions of supervision. These conditions have been read to me. I fully understand the conditions and have been provided a copy of them. It is so ordered. Marshals, come and take this man."

## Discover the Power of Your Mind and Words

I have heard some people say, "What is wrong with me? Why am I behaving this way? Why am I thinking like this? What is wrong with my mind?

You enemy's number one target is the reservoir of your mind. The enemy knows that you are controllable, and he can manipulate your whole life. Your thoughts regulate your attitude and behavior and will determine your destiny. The enemy doesn't know what you are thinking, but what you do tells the tale.

Live in harmony with one another. Don't be haughty and conceited. Associate yourselves with humble people, those with a realistic self-view. Never repay anyone evil for evil. Take thought for what you know is right and proper in the sight of everyone. When I elevate my mind, I go higher in the LORD. A person with a carnal mind will not do right. To be carnally minded is death. The one with a spiritual mind has life and peace. For a carnal-minded person is an enemy against GOD. This mind will not be subject to the laws of GOD. When you elevate your mind, the peace of GOD that passes all understanding will keep your hearts and minds through JESUS CHRIST.

Let us think on things that are true, things that are honest, things that are just pure, things that are lovely, things that are of a good report. If we do, we will be praise and found to be virtuous. So regulate your mind and go higher.

## Regulate Your Mind and Go Higher

Most times, we concocted things in our minds, and convolute with others to make ourselves look good, but the intent is to deceive.

We will either bring it out ourselves, or GOD will cause the intent that He knows to be revealed.

> Simon Peter asked Ananias this question: "Why have you allowed Satan to fill your heart to lie to the Holy Ghost, to keep back part of the price of the land? Didn't it belong to you before it was sold? And after it was sold, wasn't the money at your disposal? Why has thou conceived this thing in thine heart? You have not lied to just human beings but to GOD." And Ananias, hearing these words, fell down dead. (Acts 5:3–5)

Your worst enemy is yourself. Therefore, you must guard your heart with diligence, for everything you do flows from the mind. If I see something I need but cannot afford to buy, I could ask someone for help or do without it. If I allow the spirit of greed to take root, I will destroy you, kill you, and then steal from you. Or in the process of stealing, I will be destroyed and kill myself, thinking that my only way to get ahead is to do that which is evil and wrong, not knowing that for every action, there is a reaction.

If you would just ask, you would not have to suffer pain or lose your life. Why should you die before your time? If you really love your life and have a desire to continue to see some good days, work hard, keep your tongue from evil. Your mind is a powerful thing to waste. For He who made the mind is the one that search the heart.

It's no wonder the songwriter penned this: "Search me O GOD, and know my heart. Try me dear Savior, and know my thoughts I pray. See if there be any wicked ways in me. Cleanse me from all my sins and set me free." As the earth is the place where things grow, so is the heart and mind. If you are always gravitating to negative thoughts, you will attract negative people, attitudes, and lifestyles. Your life is a testimony of your thoughts. Just as magnet attracts magnet, we constantly draw in the things we think about. Emotions are affected by our thoughts. The way we think is the way we feel.

You will be jovial and happy if you think happy thoughts. As a man thinks in his heart, so is he.

> And the LORD will take away from thee all sickness, and will put none of the evil diseases of Egypt, which you know, upon you. If you say in your heart, these nations are more than I, how can I dispossess them? Thou shall not be afraid of them: but shall well remember what the LORD thy GOD did unto Pharaoh, and unto all Egypt. (Deut. 7:15–18)

> Thou shall remember all the way which the LORD thy GOD led thee these forty years in the wilderness, to humble thee, and prove thee, to know what was in thine heart, whether thou wouldest keep His commandments, or not. And He humbled thee, and suffered thee to hunger, and fed thee with manna, which thou knowest not, neither did thy fathers know; that He might make thee know that man does not live by bread alone, but by every word that proceedeth out of the mouth of the LORD man live. Thy raiment waxed not old upon you, neither did your foot swell, these forty years. Thou shall also consider in thine heart, that as a man chasens his sons, so the LORD thy GOD chasens thee. Therefore thou shall keep the LORD's commandments to walk in His ways and love Him. For the LORD brings thee into a good land of brooks, water, fountains, and depts that spring up out of valleys and hills. A land of wheat and barley, vines, fir trees, pome-granates, olive oil, and honey. a land in which thou shall eat bread without scarceness, thou shall not lack anything in it, a land whose stones

are iron, and out of whose hills thou mayest dig brass.

When thou has eaten and are full, thou shall bless the LORD thy GOD for the good land that He has given thee. Beware that you forget not the LORD GOD, in keeping His commandments, and His judgment, and His statues.

Lest when thou has eaten and are full, and has built godly houses to live in, and your herds and flocks multiplied, and all that thou has is multiplied, then thine heart be lifted up, you forget the LORD thy GOD which brought thee forth out of the land of Egypt, from the house of bondage. Who led thee through that great and terrible wilderness, wherein were fiery serpents, scorpions, and droughts, where there was no water; who brought thee forth water out of the rock of flint. Who fed thee with manna, which thy fathers did not know, that He might humble thee, and prove thee, to do thee good at the end; and thou shall say in thine heart, "My power and my might has gotten me this wealth."

But thou shall remember the LORD thy GOD: for it He that giveth thee power to get wealth, that He may establish His covenant which He sware unto thy fathers. (Deut. 8)

## The Liar

The enemy will offer you things to control your lifestyle. The devil took JESUS to a very high mountain for a test and showed Him all the kingdoms of the world and their splendor. "All this will I give you," he said, "If you will bow down and worship me." If you make the mistake and listen to the enemy and the good offer he makes and start dwelling on them, he will control your actions and your emotions. You will lose your thought to GOD and want nothing to do with Him. The enemy wants to sit on the throne of your heart and mind as GOD. To whom you allow yourself to obey, that's whose servant you are.

The enemy will come at you from every angle and all direction to hamper the progress of your heart and mind. The more you dwell on the enemy's lies, the more trash he brings in if you allow him. Therefore, it is paramount for us to guard our hearts diligently.

You will be discouraged and depressed, and your life will seem to have no meaning. Your life will seem to be tough sometimes and take a toll on you, for all of us are prone to the enemy's attack and his lies. No one can make you depressed! You choose to be depressed! If you are happy, that's good. No one can force you to be happy.

If you have a bad attitude and you are negative, no one is compelling you to be bored, sarcastic, or swellheaded. You can choose to remain in that condition or allow yourself to be released. Take responsibility for your own actions. As long as we keep on making excuses and blaming others, the devil, GOD, and family, we will never be free and emotionally healthy. Our attitudes determine our altitude. "I am not blessed. I am so sad, no one to care, no place to go." But there are many places to go. All we have to do is choose the right place and do the right thing. But how do I know what is right? Just fear (honor) the LORD, and you will know what is right.

If men or women entice you to do the wrong thing, don't give into them. If they say, "Come along with us, we are going to take matters into our hands. Let us ambush some harmless soul. Let us swallow them alive like the grave, then we will get all sorts of valuable things and fill our houses. We will share the loot." My friends, don't go along with them. Out in the open, GOD's wisdom speaks loud and clear.

Some folks have told me, "You don't understand what we are going through. Circumstances and hard times have taken a toll on us." It is the thought about the circumstances that have you down, not the circumstances. "I am at my wits end. I believe I'm at the point of no return." Just ask the Savior to help you and to comfort, strengthen, and keep you. He is willing to help you, and He will see you through. Whatever you put your mind to do, you can, for it is the LORD GOD who strengthens you so you can think and to be in the know.

## See Yourself as a Champion

I am a champion. That's how I see myself. I am a winner. It makes no difference how many times I've lost; I will focus on my winnings. I am a victor, not a victim. I am not weak; I am strong. I don't look at the giants; I see myself as a giant. See yourself as a fighter, not a failure. Don't you be a whiner, be a winner.

Just be careful what you are allowing your mind to dwell on. Will you focus on your problems? Are you dwelling constantly on the negative things? The way you view your life makes all the difference in this world. You cannot avoid problems or live in denial, pretending that nothing bad has ever happened to us. Let us be realistic. Since the creation, bad things happen to good people and good things happen to bad people. To pretend is not the answer. You will receive the answer when you learn to pray. Let us pray and not pretend.

## Caleb the Giant

The children of Judah came unto Joshua in Gilgal: and Caleb the son of Jephunneh the Kenezite said unto him, "Thou knowest the thing that the LORD said unto Moses the man of GOD concerning me and thee in Kadesh-barnea. Forty years old I was when Moses the servant of the LORD sent me from Kadesh-barnea to spy out the land; I brought him words again as it was in my heart. But my brethren that went up with me made the heart of the people melt: but I wholly followed the LORD my GOD.

Moses sware in that day, saying, "Surely the land whereon thy feet have trodden shall be thine inheritance, and thy children's forever, because thou had wholly followed the LORD my GOD." And now, behold, the LORD has kept me alive, as He said, these 45 years, since the LORD spake this word unto Moses, while the children of Israel wandered in the wilderness. Look, I am this day 85 years old. I am as strong this day as I was in the day that Moses sent me for war, both to go out, and to come in.

Now therefore, give me this mountain, whereof the LORD spake in that day; for thou heard in that day how the (giants) Anakims were there, and the cities were great and fenced: if so be, the LORD will be with me, then I will be able to drive out the giants, as He has said.

Joshua blessed Caleb the son of Jephunneh and gave him Hebron for an inheritance because he wholly followed the LORD GOD of Israel. (Josh. 14:6-14).

## Caleb's victory

So Caleb, the son of Jephunneh, went up to Hebron and drove out the three sons of the giant Anak, Sheshai, Ahiman, and Talmi (Josh. 15:14). The weak must say, "I am strong."

"I am as strong this day as I was in the day Moses sent me for war, both to go out, and to come in," Caleb said.

# David's Victory

In the days of King Saul, Israel was at war. The Philistines stood on one side of the mountain, and Israel on the other side, a valley was between them. The Philistines and their giant defied the armies of GOD.

The giant, Goliath, taunted Israel morning and evening; and they were afraid. David, the youngest son of Jesse, had returned from Saul, the king, to feed his father's sheep in Bethlehem. So Jesse said to David, his son, "Come here my son take this food down to the war for your brothers." David rose up early in the morning, and he left the sheep with a keeper and went as his father had commanded him.

As David approached, he noticed that the battle was in disarray, and he saluted his brothers. As he talked with them, the champion, Goliath by name, approached them from out of the Philistines army. And all the men of Israel, when they saw the man, fled from him and were so afraid. They all said, "Have you seen this man that is come up? He is here to defy Israel. The man that kill him, the king will make him rich, and give him his daughter, and make his father's house free in Israel."

When David heard the words of the men, he said, "What shall be done for the men that kills the Philistine, and take away the reproach from Israel? Who is this uncircumcised Philistine, that he should defy the armies of the living GOD? I will go and fight with this Philistine."

His words were told to King Saul, and Saul sent for him to confirm his words. King Saul told David, "You are not yet able to go against this Philistine to fight him."

## David's testimony

David said to King Saul, "Your servant kept his father's sheep, and there came a lion, and a bear, and took a lamb out of the flock. I went out after him, and smote him, and delivered the lamb out of his mouth. When he rose against me, I caught him by the beard, and smote him, and slew him. Thy servant slew both the lion and the bear. This uncircumcised Philistine shall be as one of them, seeing he has defied the armies of the living GOD. Moreover, the LORD that delivered me out of the paws of the lion and out of the paws of the bear. He will deliver me out of the hands of this Philistine."

Then said Saul unto David, "Go, and the LORD be with you."

David went out to face the giant. When the Philistine saw the boy, David, he disdained him and cursed him by his gods.

The Philistine said to David, "Am I a dog that you come to me with sticks? Come to me, and I will give your flesh unto the fowls of the air and the beast of the field."

## *The giant is defeated*

Then said David to the Philistine, "You come to me with sword, spear, and a shield. I come against you in the name of the LORD of hosts, the GOD of the armies of Israel, whom you have defied. This day will the LORD deliver thee into my hands. I will smite you and take your head from your body. I will give the carcasses of the host of the Philistines this day unto the fowls of the air and to the beast of the earth, that all the earth may know that there is a GOD in Israel. All this assembly will know that He saveth not with sword and spear, the battle is the LORD's and He will deliver you into our hands."

As the giant came to meet David, this ruddy-looking boy ran toward the army to meet the champ. He put his hand in his bag and took out one of the five stones and put it in the sling and shot the giant in the forehead, and he fell to the ground dead. David ran and stood upon the giant and took his sword out of the sheath and cut off his head with it. And when the Philistines saw that their champion was dead, they fled.

# Let Your Mind and Words Defeat Your Giant

Just think on numerous occasions someone said to you, "You can't do that!" But then you pressed ahead, trying very hard to prove them wrong. You convince yourself that you can. "I will defeat this giant, I know I can."

Your parents and some family members told you that you are no good. You respond "Everything that GOD made was very good."

They say you are a failure. You say, "I'm striving to go further. I will see you in the future."

You are so lazy, they said. You prove them wrong by working very hard.

You messed up and dropped out of school. Don't give up, start over. Find a curriculum that suits your needs and pursue it. Remember, you can do all things through CHRIST who strengthens you.

They said you have trouble on every side. You say, "I am not distressed."

They said you are perplexed, that you are in a slum. But you say, "I'm not in despair."

They said you don't understand. You say, "Yes, I do."

Folks whose minds are blind will not see what you see. Only the LORD can show you what no eyes have seen. Seeing then that we have so much hope, let us use great plainness. Put GOD first and watch Him as He leads you in the way you go and in the way you should go.

When folks disparaged you with their words, saying, "You are naughty and full of pride." Say like David, "What have I now done? Is there not a cause?" In other words, I'll show you that I am not full of pride or have been naughty, but when I am through, you will see and understand.

## Demonstrating Your Mind Words

The first place you must win the victory is in your mind. If you don't think you can be successful, you never will be. If you don't think you are a winner, you will not win. If you think your words mean nothing, you are disillusioned. For by your words are justified, and by your words you are condemned. If you don't think GOD can help you, He probably won't. When you think thoughts of failure, you are destined to fail. If you think you are sick, you are. But the sick must say, "I am healed."

When blind Bartimaeus heard the roar of the crowd, and knowing that is was JESUS, he began to shout, "JESUS, son of David, have mercy on me." Many rebuked him, told him to be quiet, but he shouted all the more, "Son of David, have mercy on me."

JESUS stopped and said, "Call him."

So they called the blind man. "Cheer up! Get on your feet! The Master is calling for you."

So he threw his cloak aside. He jumped to his feet and came to JESUS.

"What do you want Me to do for you?" JESUS asked him.

The blind man said, "Rabbi, I want to see."

Jesus said, "Go your way, your faith has healed you."

Immediately, he received his sight and followed Jesus along the road.

## Speak Encouraging Words

One Friday, August of 2018, while speaking to Michael, he said, "Brother Williams, I am so frustrated. I believe I'm going to have a heart attack." Three days later, Monday afternoon another friend called and said, "Did you hear that Michael died?"

You have to speak life into your cause. When you align yourself and your thoughts with God's thoughts, you can start dwelling on the promises of His Word. When you think excellent, positive thoughts, you will be propelled into greatness. You are bound to receive God's supernatural blessings. Life and death is in your tongue. You have a choice.

## When You Think Excellent, Positive Thoughts, You Will Be Propelled into Greatness

As we speak life in our natural circumstances, we should also remember this: "He that hears the Word of God and believe in Jesus Christ has everlasting life and will not come into condemnation, but is crossed over from death unto life." If the living dead will hear the voice of Jesus, our God, they that hear will live.

## Carefully Choose Your Words, You Have a Choice

You must choose to keep your mind on higher things. In Colossians 3:2, Paul states, "Set you affection (mind) on things above." I choose to look up! Why? When I look up, I see the vastness of the universe. I can reach to higher heights. But when I look down, all that I see is right there, earth. In Psalm 121, the writer said, "I will lift mine eyes unto the hills, from whence cometh my help. My help cometh form the Lord, which made heaven and earth."

THE BEST IS YET TO COME

If you noticed, there is something that we must all do. My help is coming down from above. I made a choice to look up, anticipating my help coming down. The LORD said, "My doctrine shall drop as the rain. My speech shall distil as the dew. Just as the small rain upon the tender herb, and as the showers upon the grass. O earth, hear the words of My mouth." Doctrine is from above. Dew is from above, rain is from above, and showers are from above. All these things that I need I do believe they are coming; therefore, I am looking with anticipation.

In Deuteronomy 30:19, Moses said, "I call heaven and earth to record this day against you, that I have set before you life and death, blessing and cursing: therefore choose life, that both you and your children may live." I have made a choice to live. Let's not wait until it's too late to look up. Let's do it now.

## Let's Not Wait until It's Too Late to Look Up

Help is always available. Let's not wait until it's too late to look up for our help. That would not be good for us.

> There was a certain rich man who was clothed in purple and fine linen and lived in luxury every day. At his gate was laid a beggar named Lazarus covered with sores and longing to eat from the rich man's table. Even the dogs came and licked his sores.
>
> The time also came when the beggar died and the angels carried him to Abraham's bosom. The rich man also died and was buried. In hell, where he was in torment, he looked up and saw Abraham far away, with Lazarus in his bosom. So he called to Him, "Father Abraham, have mercy on me and send Lazarus to dip the tip of finger in water and cool my tongue, because I am in agony in this fire. (Luke 16:19–29)

You see, friends, this man had enough time to ask for help from Father Abraham. He waited until he was in hell to lift up his eyes and requested help. There is no repentance in the grave. No pardon will be given to a dead man. Today, if you hear the voice of GOD calling you to repentance, do not harden your heart.

> And there shall be signs in the sun, and upon the earth distress of the nations with perplexity, while the sea with waves roaring. Men's heart failing them because they are fearful, and apprehensive of what will be coming on earth, for the heavenly bodies will be shaken. At that time you will see the Son of Man coming in a cloud with power and great glory. When these things begin to take place, then look up, and lift up your heads, because your redemption is drawing near. (Luke 21:25–28)

Friends, look up and believe in JESUS CHRIST who is able to save you to the utmost. He will not force you. But if you need GOD's help and you are striving to be that person He wants you to be, you ought to line up your vision with His. Learn to look and live with a positive frame of mind. JESUS CHRIST is your life. You are dead without Him.

## Let Us Look Up and Believe in JESUS CHRIST, Who Is Able to Save You to the Utmost

> Look unto Me, JESUS, and be saved, all the ends of the earth: for I am GOD, there is none else. I have sworn by myself. My Word is gone out of My mouth in righteousness, and shall not return; that unto (Me) JESUS, every knee shall bow and every tongue shall confess. (Isa. 45:22–23)

> And the LORD said unto Moses, "Make thee a fiery serpent of brass and set it upon a pole.

It shall come to pass that everyone that is bit-
ten, when he looketh up on it, shall live." (Num.
21:8)

You must make an effort to keep your mind focused on the
higher powers. Say to GOD, "My mind belongs to you. I know that
You are in control of my life." When trouble comes your way and it
seems you can't tell the night from day and you are in degradation,
you must choose to trust GOD for good things and not allow yourselves to be down and discouraged and give up.

## You Can Encourage Yourself in the LORD

As you proceed in life and genuinely set your mind to do good
and to help others, with the fear of GOD, most people will not believe
and trust you.

> The young man David that defeated the
> giant was not trusted by the Philistines. But
> David had a friend whose name was Achish, and
> he gave David a place to stay for one year and
> four months because he found no fault in him.
>
> The princes of the Philistines thought
> otherwise.
>
> They asked Achish, "Who is this?"
>
> "David, the servant of Saul," he replied.
>
> The princes were not pleased with him.
> Then they said, "Make this fellow return and go
> back to the place you has appointed for him lest
> in the heat of the battle he become an adversary
> to us."
>
> Then Achish called David and said to
> him, "Surely as the LORD lives, thou has been
> upright, going out and coming in with me. I
> have found no evil in thee: nevertheless the lords
> of the Philistines don't trust you. Wherefore now

2222.

return, and go in peace, that thou displease them not."

David said to Achish, "What have I done? Why can't I go and fight against the enemies of my lord the king?"

Achish said to David, "I know you are a good man in my sight, as an angel of GOD, nevertheless the princes of the Philistines have said, 'You shall not go up with us to the battle.' As soon as you rise in the morning and have light, please depart."

David did.

(1 Sam. 29)

It took David and his men three days to return to Ziklag, where he had resided. When he got there, the Amalekites invaded the south, and Ziklag, they burned with fire. They took all the women and David's two wives. The men that were with David lifted up their voices and wept until they were weak.

David was distressed greatly because his men spoke of stoning him, but David encouraged himself in the LORD, his GOD.

## Inquiring mind wants to know

King David and the priest Abisthar prayed. David inquired of the LORD, saying, "Shall I pursue after this troop? Will I overtake them?" The LORD said, "Pursue! Thou shall surely overtake them and recover all without fail." So David proceeded as the LORD said to him and recovered all that the Amalekites had carried away.

David had two hundred men who were faint and weary. They did not go with him to the recovery. They came out to meet the king, and when he came near, he saluted them. But the evil men and troublemakers among David's followers said, "Because they did not go out with us, we will not share with them the plunder we recovered. However, each may take his wife and his children and go." Then said David, "No, my brothers, you must not do that with what the LORD has given us. He has protected us and handed over to us the forces that came against us. Who will listen to you in this matter? The share of the man who stayed with the supplies is to be the same as that of him who went down to the battle. All will share alike." And David made this a statue and an ordinance for Israel from that day up to now.

## Get Rid of Those Crazy Thoughts

When your thoughts begin to run in a certain direction for a long period of time, it is as though you have a trench and it's been taken over by a river and the water flows in only one direction. So it is with a person who habitually thinks negatively, week after week, month after month. Your negative thoughts dig the trench deeper and deeper. Now the flow of the river gets faster and faster and wider. So is every thoughts that flows in and through the mind, it carries away almost everything in its way in one direction. I will not pattern my mind to think in this negative direction.

Truly, we can dig a new, bigger, wider trench going in the opposite positive direction. We do this one thought at a time by dwelling on GOD'S WORD. Now we are able to water the parched places, the roots and the base of the tree of the mind and thoughts of our mind, and we are equipped to help others.

> Blessed is the man that trust in the LORD, whose hope the LORD is. For he shall be as tree planted by the waters, and spreads out her roots by the river, and he shall not see when heat cometh, but her leaves shall be green, and not worry in the year of drought, neither shall cease from yielding her fruit. (Jer. 17:6–8)

Let us strive to keep the river trench thoughts of the mind positive. We will always be tempted to revert to the old, discouraging negative thoughts. If you can muster enough strength to think good, honest, just, lovely, and pure, you will say, "I can do better. I am better than this. GOD is with me, who can be against me?" In all these things, we are more than conquerors through Him that loved us. I will not fear, for JESUS walks beside me. I am sheltered in the arms of GOD.

Let us look at the way GOD thinks and the way the enemy thinks. The sons of GOD came to present themselves before GOD, and Satan also came with them. The LORD said to Satan, "Where are you coming from?" Satan responded, "From roaming throughout the earth, going back and forth in it." The LORD said unto Satan, "Has thou considered My servant Job? There is none like him in the earth, a perfect and upright, a man that fears GOD and shuns evil" (Job 1).

GOD's thoughts about Job is mind-boggling: *There is none like him in the earth. He's a perfect man and upright. He's one that fears GOD and stays away from evil.*

Now let us listen to the devil's crazy thoughts: *Does Job fear GOD for nothing? Has thou not put a hedge around him and his household and everything he has? Thou has blessed the work of his hands so that his flocks and herds are spread throughout the land. But now stretch out you hand and strike everything he has, and he will curse thee to thy face.*

Are you so wise that you can argue with GOD? Can you counsel GOD? The LORD our GOD said, "Job is a perfect and upright man. He fears GOD and hates evil."

After the devil's challenge, the LORD GOD said unto Satan, "Very well then, everything he has is in your power, but on the man himself do not lay your hand."

The devil said to himself, "The game is on." So the devil went out from the presence of GOD and did all the evil he thought about Job. After he took out his vengeance on GOD through Job's troubles, take a look at what Job did.

Job got up, tore his robe, and shaved his head. Then he fell to the ground and worshipped GOD and said, "Naked came I out of my mother's womb, and naked I will depart. The LORD gave, and the LORD has taken away. Blessed be the name of the LORD."

In all this, Job did not sin, nor charged GOD foolishly.

Truly, the devil was not pleased. His thoughts about Job and God blew up in his face. He said Job would curse God. But Job worshipped and blessed the name of the LORD.

GOD has not forgotten you. GOD has not given up on you. GOD will never leave you nor forsake you. When the devil comes, he's thinking how to steal from you, kill you, and destroy you. Now the thoughts of his mind are running wild. *I have to get at GOD. I have to destroy Job. I have to prove GOD He's wrong*, the devil thought (Job 2).

Again, there was a day when the sons of GOD came to present themselves before the LORD, and Satan came also among them to present himself before the LORD. And the LORD said unto Satan, "From where have you come?"

Satan answered the LORD, "From roaming around the earth, and from walking up and down in it."

The LORD said to Satan, "Have you considered My servant Job? For there is none like him on the earth, a blameless and upright man? He fears GOD with reverence and abstains from and turns away from evil because he honors GOD? And still he maintains and holds tightly to his integrity although you incited Me against him to destroy him without a cause?"

Satan answered the LORD, "Skin for skin! Yes, a man will give all he has for his life. But put forth Your hand now and touch his bone and his flesh (and afflict him severely), and he will curse You to Your face."

My brothers, sisters, and all you lovely and wonderful people who will read this book, have you ever did things differently from what is right? I will be the first to say yes, I have thought differently and did it my way. I have proven myself wrong all the time. Get rid of those crazy thoughts.

So the LORD said to Satan, "Behold, he is in your hand, only spare his life."

Satan departed from GOD's presence. He went and struck Job with loathsome boils and agonizingly painful soars from the sole of his foot to the crown of his head. Now Job found himself in a very precarious situation. He needs help. He needs someone to show empathy and to sympathize with him.

Now let's look at what happened.

Then said his wife to him, "Are you still clinging to your integrity and your faith and trust in GOD without blaming Him? Curse GOD and die!"

But Job said unto his wife, "You speak as one of the foolish women speaks. Shall we accept only good from GOD and not also accept adversity and disaster?"

In spite of all the things that happened to Job, he did not sin with words from his lips.

The enemy said, "He will curse You to Your face."

His wife said, "Curse GOD and die!"

GOD said, "Job is perfect in spirit. He's still holding to his integrity, although you moves me to destroy him without a cause."

Just ask yourself this question: many people are dying before their time, why should you die before your time?

With your foolish thoughts, you can go ahead, curse GOD, and die. I will bless the LORD at all times. His praise shall always be in my mouth. I have forsaken my wicked ways. Now that I am walking righteously, I have changed my thoughts. The LORD JESUS CHRIST had mercy on me and abundantly pardoned me. I got rid of those crazy thoughts. I will always be positive. When I plant and sow, I will reap. If I seek, I will find. If I knock, the door will open to me. If I ask with the right attitude, I will receive. If I fall and can't get up by myself, I will call out for help. When I am afflicted, I will pray. When I am sick, I will ask for prayer that I may be healed. And if I sin, I will be forgiven. I rid myself of those crazy thoughts. Come on, let's do it. You can.

After man sinned, GOD, not willing that any should perish, gave man 969 years to repent and have a change of heart and feel and seek for him. But He saw man's evil heart, that they had no desire to seek for His mercy, so He reduced man's time on earth.

"Do not be like the horse or the mule, which have no understanding, but must be controlled by bit and bridle, or they will not come to you" (Ps. 32:9). If at all you have GOD on your mind and you know that without Him you are dead, don't hide your iniquity and acknowledge your sins. He will grant you mercy. He is GOD. He will abundantly pardon you. But if you refuse and rebel, you will be devoured by the sword (His Word).

## You Are Still Here

The fact that you are still here, GOD is not through with you. GOD is not finish with you. You have a lot for GOD to work on for you. Truth is, you are very scared. You should be grateful that he has kept you living this long so that He can work on you. We know if we're honest with ourselves to say, "If it had not been for GOD's mercy, forever, our souls would be lost." He has His eyes on you. Can't you see! He has you in His grasp.

But GOD commendeth His love toward us, in that, while we were yet sinners, CHRIST died for us (Rom. 5:8).

Don't try to impress GOD. Come to GOD. "He will have mercy and abundantly pardon you."

# DEVELOP A SELF-IMAGE THAT IS HEALTHY

## Who Are You?

Only fourteen years old, Norman, who became blind, should not have made it. This young man, whose father was also blind, was very inspirational in his actions. What Norman wanted to become was now in question. To be this young and blind had its disadvantages. Some people laughed at his blindness as he navigates his way with a stick. Some people are very inconsiderate with those with disabilities. Norman was very courageous and had a will to survive. He said, "While there is a will there is a way." Despite the factors working against him, Norman persevered. He turned to farming, for he said, "I refused to be dependent on family and others." So he started farming, planting different crops, namely, bananas, potatoes, corn, carrots, and cabbage. This has been very challenging for Norman, but he was determined to be independent. He choose to make it, working very hard, going through bushes, dew, rocks, and long distance. But he said, "My survival depends on me." He sold his cabbage, which was the main source of his income. He said life is a challenge and that life is sweet. We can achieve anything that we put our minds to. GOD has placed in us the power of the mind: determination. I know I can make it if I put the effort into what I do, or intend to do.

Norman has also written many songs for over thirty years, which he intends to record. He said most of his songs are classics. He had a harmonious voice, and he plays the piano. This young man is very encouraging. He encourages young men to put away guns and stop the destruction of their brothers and sisters. He said, "We are a healthy people and a healthy nation if we can see ourselves in this way. We are better than this. We should give thanks and praise to the Father, who has endowed us with many blessings and talents." He is making news on social media and hopes to take it like a storm, for things are getting better.

# A Self-Image That Is Healthy

What does GOD's WORD says about me? It's all up to me! Some people base their self-image on the neighborhood they live in, the model and style of the cars they drive, the restaurants they dine in, the stores they shop, and those who advises them. How you feel about yourself and see yourself will impact your progress in life and whether or not you fulfill your destiny. "We are laborers together with GOD; we are GOD's field; we are GOD's building."

# We Are Laborers Together with GOD

Do you know that GOD is truly wonderful. His understanding is infinite. We are laborers together with GOD. And GOD said, "Let us make man in our image, after our likeness." So, in GOD's image, He created male and female. He blessed them and said, "Be fruitful and multiply." My mother and father labored in the flesh, and I came forth. As I grew and begin my exploration, I realized that a life without GOD is futile and vain.

You should not base your self-image on the number of men or women you sleeps with. The body is more than meat. It is more than just good looks and the raiment you wear. The body is a building and needs proper care. You do your part and the LORD will do His part. Your social status means nothing. Wherever we are from and wherever we go, we should be concerned about others and not just to please ourselves. I esteem GOD and lift Him up, giving Him glory and praise. This is what I am expecting from GOD and man.

I am doing the best I can, shooting for the stars. As I go, I begin to say, "I never do anything right." But then I met a friend and told him my plans. He began to praise me, saying, "That is a good idea. I know you can do it. Go ahead and shoot for the stars, and do not allow anyone to hinder you." My self-image got healthy after hearing these words.

Do not praise yourself; let someone else do it. The praise should come from a stranger and not from your own mouth.

THE BEST IS YET TO COME


"I have found David, the son of Jesse, a man after mine own heart, he shall fulfill my will."

In Damascus, there was a disciple name Ananias. The LORD called to him in a vision.

"Ananias!"

"Yes, LORD," he answered.

"Go to the house of Judas on Straight Street and ask for a man from Tarsus name Saul, for he is praying. In a vision, he has seen a man named Ananias come and place his hands on him to restore his sight," the LORD said.

"LORD," Ananias answered, "I have heard many reports about this man and all the harm he has done to your holy people in Jerusalem. And he has come here with authority form the chief priests to arrest all who call on Your name."

"Go! This man is a chosen vessel to proclaim My name to the Gentiles and their kings and to the people of Israel. I will show him how must he must suffer for My name."

Ananias went to the house and entered it. Seeing Saul, he placed his hand on him and said, "Brother Saul, the LORD JESUS (GOD), who appeared to you on the road as you were coming here, has sent me so that you may see again and be filled with the Holy Spirit."

Immediately, something like scales fell from Saul's eyes, and he could see again. He got up and was baptized in the name of JESUS CHRIST. JESUS saw Nathanael coming toward Him and said, "Here is a true man of Israel in whom there is no deceit" (John 1:47).

"For if a man thinks himself to be something, when he is nothing, he deceives himself." Do you see yourself as a building of GOD? Will you allow Him to use you in a healthy, positive way? GOD wants us to have healthy, positive self-image and to see ourselves as priceless treasures. "And GOD saw everything that he had made, and behold, it was very good." He wants us to feel good about ourselves when He changed us from the inside. But if we allow ourselves to do that which is right in our own eyes, it's no longer us but sin that dwells in us.

"But in a great house there are not only vessels of gold and silver but of wood and earth and some to honor and dishonor." Put away profanity from out of your mouth and let the Word of GOD dwells in you in all wisdom. Today, all that we see is lust that affects our eyes and our flesh. We boast and are proud about it. If you stay away from youthful lust, build up your faith in GOD, be kind in your affections to one another with brotherly love, you are doing well. If you learn to follow peace with everyone and strive to do that which is right, you do well. If you clean up the building (our body), you will be honorable vessels, sanctified, prepared for GOD to do every good work. Your self-image is not the physical part of your body. It is your spirit man that controls your actions and your performance.

GOD is spirit and flesh. Therefore, He made man and breathed into him the breath of life; and man became a living soul, spirit, and flesh. When Adam sinned and the LORD GOD called to him, "Adam! Where are you?"

Adam said, "I heard your voice walking in the garden. I was afraid because I was naked, and I hid myself."

And the LORD GOD said to Adam, "Who told thee that thou was naked? Has thou eaten of the tree whereof I commanded thee thou should not eat?"

Adam's self-image changed. Now Adam sees himself as naked.

## I See Myself a Naked Man

From the day that GOD formed man and breathed life into him and he became a living soul, he was naked. When he sinned, he saw himself differently. I thought I was right, now I found out I am so wrong. What shall I do? Sin makes us naked spiritually. Now they wanted to be different, the man and his wife. They sewed fig leaves together and made themselves aprons. They had enough time to do their own invention, and so they did. There is a way that seems right unto man, but the end of its way is death.

The LORD GOD was not pleased with the images He had made and what He saw because of sin. Therefore, the LORD GOD shed the blood of an animal and made coats of skins and clothed them. GOD's way is always right. "For My ways are not your ways, and My thought are not your thoughts," said the LORD. Before they sinned, they were naked yet having fellowship with GOD. Now that they disobeyed and sinned against GOD, they clothed themselves. But before they sinned, the man and his wife were naked and not ashamed. Now they saw themselves clothed and driven out of the garden, where they had fellowship with the LORD. They took on themselves the old man and his evil deeds. Fellowship with the LORD was no longer available. The body (building) is now occupied by the deceiver, trickster, and the father of lies.

## They Took on Themselves the Old Man and His Evil Deeds

When I repented of my sins and got baptized in water, in the name of JESUS CHRIST, I died. I hid myself (my life) in CHRIST in GOD. But I still make myself as earthly good to fulfill my purpose in life.

> And now you also put off all these: Anger, wrath, malice, blasphemy, filthy communication out of your mouth. Lie not one to another, seeing that you have put off the old man with his deeds; and have put on the new man which is renewed in knowledge after the image of GOD that created him. (Col. 3:8–10)

## A Reconciled Image

As a foreigner who goes to a new country and goes through the rudiments of becoming a citizen, he or she has been adopted. All the benefits and privileges are available to you. In the same way, when you make that change and turn to GOD, who is JESUS CHRIST, the LORD, because of His slain body, you have been reconciled. Before this transformation, you, who were sometime alienated and enemies in your mind because of wicked works, a new image has been created. I am now walking in JESUS CHRIST, whom I have received. I am rooted and built up in JESUS CHRIST and established in my faith, giving thanks to GOD for my citizenship and the promise of my new country.

There is a process we all have to go through, and it takes time. As I see in this great country, people from all walks of life are hazarding their lives through bushes, in water, over walls, and sun-baked containers just to get to this place. Some said they took the journey because of political persecution and are searching for a better life. Others said they have been told by Joe Biden to come. So they are corning, jumping ahead of those who have been in the process and are waiting for their time.

But with GOD, this is different. He is calling those who have labored and are laboring in sin to come. GOD is not doing this because of political gratification. He calls us because He loves us. No one else is able to help us but Him. He will be coming back for His reconciled people. That where He is, there will we be also.

In old times, those who have not received the promises of GOD were encouraged by what they heard and embraced them. They confessed with their mouths that they were pilgrims and strangers on the earth. Plainly said, they were seeking for a better country, a heavenly country, for GOD has prepared for them a city. If all that we are craving and hoping for are earthly natural things, we are a people most miserable.

I migrated from Jamaica in 1980 because of the political instability at that time. People were killing, looting, stealing, and committing all kinds of violence against their own people. When I got here, I noticed the same things happening here. Some people sees themselves as second-class citizens: overworked, underpaid, and treated like slaves. So they started the blame game, the race game, and the imagination of their thoughts and hearts grew evil. So they go about to make things better by looting, killing, drugging, stealing as their foolish heart's desire. They do not understand that as a man thinks in his heart and mind, so is he.

Now the LORD had said to Abraham, "Get thee out of thy country, from thy kinfolks, to a land I will shew thee." So Abraham departed as the LORD had spoken. And they went forth to go into the land of Canaan. Into the land of Canaan, they came. Abraham was called a friend of GOD because he believed. GOD saved me by His grace, that in the ages to come He might show the incomparable riches of His grace toward us. He has made known unto us the mystery of His will according to His good pleasure. I am not just a foreigner or as one seeking refuge; I am a citizen with GOD's people, also a member of His household.

Since my arrival in this country, I have moved from city to city. "For here we have no lasting city, but I am seeking that city which is to come." For GOD said, "I go to prepare a place for you. You know the way to the place where I am going, and if I go and prepare a place for you, I will come back and take you with me, that you also may be where I am."

## You Know You Are a Man

So who are you for real? Let us explore to find out the truth, the whole truth, and nothing but the truth. "In the day that GOD created man, in the likeness of GOD the man was made; male and female created He them; and GOD bless them, and called their name Adam." GOD created a healthy man (male). He created a healthy woman (female). "The LORD GOD brought her unto him (the man)." And Adam said, "This is now bone of my bones, and flesh of my flesh: she shall be called woman, because she was taken out of man. Therefore, shall a man leave his father and mother and cleave unto his wife," and they became one flesh. They were both naked, the man and his wife. They were not ashamed.

After they sinned, GOD came and called, "Adam, where are you?"

Adam said, "I heard Your voice in the garden, and I was afraid. Because I was naked, I hid myself."

"Who told you that? Has thou eaten of the tree whereof I commanded thee that thou should not eat?"

And the man said, "The woman you gave me to be with me, she gave me of the tree, and I did eat." Adam confessed to GOD, saying, "You gave me a woman to be with me. She gave to me from the tree, and I did eat." And Adam called his wife's name Eve because she was the mother of all living.

Adam knew his wife, and she conceived and bore Cain. He slept with his wife, and they had coition. After nine months of gestation, Eve gave birth to a baby boy. They named him Cain. Again, she became pregnant and gestated for nine months and gave birth to another baby boy. They called him Abel. Adam was 130 years old when he slept with his wife and got a son in his own image and his likeness, and he named him Seth. After Seth was born, Adam lived 800 years and had other sons and daughters (emphasis on sons and daughters, boys and girls) (Gen. 4).

In Genesis 16:11–12, the angel of the LORD said unto her, "Behold, thou are with child (pregnant), and shall bear a son (give birth), and shall call his name Ishmael; he will be a wild man. Genesis 17:5 says, "Neither shall thy name any more be called Abram, but that name shall be Abraham, for a father of nations have I made thee." Question: Do you know you are a man? In verse 15–16, GOD said to Abraham, "As for Sarai thy wife, thou shall not call her name Sarai, but Sarah shall be her name. I will bless her, and give thee a son also of her. Yes, I will bless her, and she shall be a mother of nations kings of people shall be of her." In verse 19, GOD said, "Sarah thy wife shall bear thee a son indeed; thou shall call his name Isaac." Do you know you are a man?

Isaac was forty years old when he married Rebekah, the daughter of Bethuel, the Syrian of Paddan-aram. Isaac prayed to the LORD for his wife because she was unable to conceive children. The LORD granted his prayer, and Rebekah, Isaac's wife, conceived twins, who struggled together within her, kicking and shoving one another. When her days to be delivered were fulfilled, behold, there were twins in her womb. The first came out reddish all over like a hairy garment. They named him Esau. Afterward, his brother came out, his hand grasping his brother's heel, and they named him Jacob.

Don't fool yourself! You know you were born a boy. You grow up to be a man. First Corinthians 13:11–12 says, "When. I was a child, I spake as a child, I act as a child, I understand as a child, I thought as a child; but when I became a man, I put away childish things (I put the ways of childhood behind me). For now you only see a reflection of yourself in a mirror." Get rid of your crazy thoughts.

The heart is deceitful above all things and beyond cure. Who can understand it? "I, the LORD, search the heart and examine the mind, to reward each person according to their conduct and deeds."

The word of the LORD came to Jeremiah, saying, "Before I formed thee in the womb I knew you. Before you were born I set you apart; I appointed you a prophet to the nations."

Then said I, "Ah, LORD, I cannot speak, I am a child."

But the LORD said to me, "Do not say, I am a child. You must go to everyone I send you to and say whatever I command you. Do not be afraid of them, for I am with you and will rescue you."

Let's be honest, and let us reason together. We all have heard people saying, "Stop lying! Will you be honest and speak the truth?" We all want to hear the truth, right? When the truth is known and spoken, what if some don't believe? Will their unbelief make the Word of GOD untrue? (I speak as a man; a man is who I am).

"Ask and see. Can a man bear children? Then why do I see every strong man with his hands on his stomach like a woman in labor, and every face turned deadly pale?" said the LORD GOD (Jer. 30:6). "A woman giving birth to a child has pain because her time has come, but as soon as she is delivered of the child, she forgets the anguish because of her joy that a child is born into the world," said JESUS.

Keep on lying to yourself. It doesn't matter how hard you try, you won't be able to give birth. My GOD is true. You are a liar. "I will greatly multiply thy sorrow and thy conception; in sorrow thou shall bring forth children; thy desire shall be for thy husband," said the LORD GOD to Eve.

We are talking about a self-image that is healthy. GOD brought Eve to Adam. But Eve believed the serpent's lies and sin with her husband. Their eyes were now opened to sin and death. Their self-image changed, and they went into hiding, having no more fellowship with GOD. But GOD is full of compassion and pity. He suffered long and waited for the right time in the garden. The LORD GOD said to the (man) Adam, "Where are you?" Adam did not say, "LORD, I have sinned. Please forgive me." But he said, "The woman You gave me to be with, she gave me of the tree, and I did eat. I found out that, I was naked and I hid myself." They, Adam and Eve, hid from God, not Adam and Steve.

# A Healthy Marriage

The Pharisees came unto Him, tempting Him, saying, "Is it lawful for a man to put away his wife for every cause?" Jesus answered, "Have you not read, that He which made them in the beginning made them male and female?" (Matt. 19).

How can a man call another man my husband? Or how can a woman call another woman my wife? Now let's be honest. You know what you are doing isn't right. You know your relationship is not healthy. Both men will not be able to produce children. Your heart is evil and is waxing worst and worst. You are living a licentious lifestyle. A man shall not have sexual relation with man as one does with a woman. It is an abomination (Lev. 18:22).

"But you are the ones who justify yourselves in the eyes of others, but God knows your heart. For that which men and women accept highly is an abomination in the sight of God." "Woe unto you that call evil good, and good evil, that put darkness for light, and light for darkness, that put bitter for sweet, and sweet for bitter." "For they that does wrong will be paid for their wrongs, and there is no favoritism with God."

"Wives, submit yourselves unto your own husbands. The husband is the head of the wife. Husbands, love your wives." "Let everyone of you in particular so love his wife even as himself, and the wife must respect her husband." You should not portray a fallacy that confuses the children and others. Love must be sincere. Hate that which is evil. Cling to what is good. Learn to control your thoughts.

"Mr. Williams, I hear what you are saying, but I have been living this way for a long, long time. It will not make sense to change now. I am going to hell anyway." No! You are wrong. Why are you going to hell? Who told you that you are going to hell? Have you really convinced yourself of this unhealthy place? Friends, God prepared hell for the devil and his angels and for all nations that forget

GOD. But if hell is where you desire to go, that is the choice you have made. In the beginning GOD commanded the Adams, "The day that you eat thereof you shall surely die." The LORD GOD gave them a choice. "Of every tree of the garden you may freely eat, but of the tree of knowledge of good and evil, you should not eat of it, for in the day you eat thereof, you shall surely die."

The LORD GOD gave them life, but also told them, "You will die in the day you eat of the tree of knowledge, of good, and evil." The serpent came up with a different scenario when he approached Eve. "Did GOD said, 'You should not eat of every tree of the garden'?" the serpent asked. The LORD did not say that, friends. Eve said to the serpent, "We may eat of the trees of the garden. But of the tree which is in the midst of the garden, GOD said, 'Ye shall not eat of it, neither shall ye touch it, lest you die.'" Did you notice that GOD did not say "neither shall ye touch it"? Can you see the image? The serpent said to the woman, "You shall not surely die. For GOD doth know that in the day you eat thereof, then your eyes shall be opened, and you shall be as gods, knowing good and evil." The woman saw and developed an image in her mind, and she choose her destiny. "The soul that sin it shall die."

## The image of death

In Adam, all die. For the wages of sin is death. GOD offered us eternal life. A person who has rebelled against GOD is as the serpent's sin of divination. Have you ever been stung by bees, spiders, wasps, snakes, and scorpions? The pain is severe, and sometimes it brings death. We have all seen pictures of dead people, and all of us have had someone who has died. The image was not, and is not, pleasant. We can choose to give up the power of life (eternal), or we can choose death in bondage. The word of life is in our mouth and in our hearts that we may obey them. The LORD our GOD has set before us life and good, death and evil. The LORD told us to choose life that we and our children may live. My friends, eternal life is a choice. I speak what I know and testify that which I have seen.

"For GOD so loved the world (people), that He gave His only begotten SON (Himself) that whosoever beliveth in Him (GOD) should not perish. For GOD sent not His SON (Himself) into the world to condemn the world; but that the world through His might be saved. He that believeth on Him is not condemned; he that beliveth not is condemned already, because he has not believed in the name of the only begotten SON of GOD."

Why will you choose that image condemnation?

## Why will you choose that image condemnation

"And when the woman saw that the tree was good for food, and that it was pleasant to the eyes, and the tree to be desired to make one wise, she took of the fruit thereof, and eat and gave also unto her husband with her, and he did eat. And their eyes were opened, and they knew that they were naked."

When you use subtility and lie to me, the way I respond to you lets you know that I believe your lies. The woman said to the devil, "GOD hath said, 'Ye shall not eat of it, neither shall ye touch it.'" The serpent knew she did not know the whole truth when she spoke. So the serpent said to the woman, "You shall not surely die. For GOD does know that the day you eat thereof, your eyes will be opened, and you shall be as gods knowing good and evil." The serpent called GOD a liar. But "GOD is not man, that He should lie, neither the Son of man that He repent. Does He speak and then not act? Does He promise and not fulfill?"

The woman chooses to believe the serpent's lies. She ate of the tree, and she died spiritually. She also gave some to her husband to whom GOD gave her to, and he did eat. The LORD called out to man He gave the commandment. "Adam! Where are you?" Adam never sought to be reconciled to GOD. He blamed GOD instead. He said, "The woman you gave me to be with me, she gave me of the tree, and I did eat." The LORD said to the woman, "What is this that thou have done?" The woman, who was deceived by the serpent, did not seek for reconciliation. She blamed GOD instead.

The LORD GOD drove out the man (Adam) and his wife from the garden and placed angels to protect the tree of life. For GOD said, "Behold, the man has now become like one of us to reach out his hand and take also from the tree of life and eat, and live forever." Altogether, Adam lived 930 years, and then he died the physical death. JESUS said, "The one who believes in me will live, even though they die."

JESUS castigated the scribes and Pharisees who portrayed themselves as being righteous.

They said to JESUS, "We were not born from committing fornication. We have one Father, even GOD."

Jesus answered, "If GOD were your Father, you would love Me. Why do you not understand My speech? Because you are unable to hear what I say. You are just like your father the devil, and the lust of your father you will do and are going. He was a murderer from the beginning, and did not abide in the truth, because there is no truth in him (the serpent). When he speaks a lie, he speaks of his own: For he is a liar and the father of it. And because I tell you the truth, you believe Me not, but now you seek to kill Me."

## What Is Truth?

Pilate said to JESUS, "What is truth?" (John 18:38).

When JESUS was arrested and brought to Annas, the high priest, he asked JESUS about His disciples and His doctrine (teaching).

JESUS replied, "I have spoken openly to the world. I always taught in the synagogues, or at the temple, where all the Jews come together. I said nothing in secret. Why are you questioning Me? Ask those that heard Me. My kingdom is not of this world. If it were, my servants would fight to prevent my arrest by the Jewish leaders. But now My kingdom is from another place."

"Heaven and earth will pass away, but My words will never pass away" (Matt. 24:35).

You will not be the first to pretend to be righteous. You will not be the last. You can get right with GOD now, or you can continue to be just like your father (daddy). He could not abide in the truth. For

GOD said, "He that worketh deceit shall not dwell in My house; he that tells lies shall not tarry in my sight" (Ps. 101:7).

GOD hates your lying tongue. He hates a false witness that speaks lies. Only the truth will make you free. If you want to be free, keep speaking the truth. When you have been put to the test, will you speak the truth? If you have been caught red-handed, will you be honest? Will you lie like Cain did?

And the LORD said unto Cain, "Where is your brother?"

"I know not. Am I my brother's keeper?" said Cain (Gen. 4:9).

Cain was just like the devil, his father, and so will you, unless you change.

# ENLARGE YOUR DREAM AND VISION IN GOD

## Enlarge Your Dream and Vision in God

I was born for a reason, and I have a purpose in life. I will strive to the best of my ability to be what God wants me to be. I know it won't be easy. But with God's help, I can do all things through Him that strengthens me. For the wise man fears the Lord God and departs from evil, but the fool runs into evil head-on. To depart from the snares of death is to fear the Lord, which is a fountain of life. Hell is beneath, and to depart from it is to look to the Lord above.

The angel of God, called the Son of the Morning, looked at himself. Because of his beauty, he was lifted up in pride, to his downfall. He was so arrogant in his spirit. He was kicked out of heaven to the earth, mad, wrathful, and upset. We have to guard ourselves from arrogance and pride. For in the lips of those who have not the wisdom of God is a burning fire, destroying one another. If I destroy you, I am destroying myself.

Jesus sent out seventy-two to preach and cast out evil spirits (demons). They returned with joy and said to Jesus, "Lord, even the demons submit to us in your name." He replied to them, "I saw Satan fall like lightning from heaven. I have given to you authority (power) to trample on snakes, and scorpions and to overcome all the power of the enemy. Nothing will harm you. Nevertheless, do not rejoice that the evil spirits submit to you, but rejoice that your names are written in heaven."

As the time approached for God to be taken up to heaven, Jesus was determined to go to Jerusalem. So He sent messengers to Samaria to get ready for His arrival. When Jesus arrived, the people of the Samaritan's village didn't receive Jesus. Two of Jesus's followers, James and John, when they saw the Samaritan's reaction, they asked the Lord, "Do you want us to call fire down from heaven to destroy them, just as Elijah did?" But the Lord corrected them, saying, "You don't know the kind of spirit you have. The Son of Man didn't come to destroy men's lives but to save them." If you come to the Son, you will have eternal life.

Let me ask you these questions, if you can answer me: "Who has ascended up in heaven? And who came down from heaven? Who has wrapped up the water in a garment? Who has established all the ends of the earth? What is His name, and what's the real name of His Son? He is a refuge and a shield unto those that put their trust in Him. Every word from His mouth is flawless. He told us who He is." If you now say JESUS is not GOD, and He said, "When you see Me, you see the Father." Do not add to His words. He will rebuke you and prove you to be a liar just like your father, the devil.

GOD, the LORD, put on righteousness as His clothing; and justice is what He wears as a robe. He is eyes to the blind and feet to the lame. He is a Father to the needy. He cares for the sick, the strangers, the weak, and the wicked. JESUS is sovereign LORD. He made heaven and earth by His great power and outstretched arms and everything that is in them. His eyes are open to the ways of all humans. He will reward each person according to their conduct and as their deeds deserve. He performed signs and wonders in Egypt and has continued them until this day, in Israel and among all mankind. He brought His people out of Egypt by signs and wonders He did to Pharaoh on the land and in the sea.

The great LORD GOD gave the children of Israel, whom He delivered their own land that He promised to give to their ancestors, a land flowing with honey and milk. They went in and took possession of it, but they did not follow or obey His law, so He brought disaster upon them. But when they cry unto GOD in their trouble, He brought them out of their distresses. We ought to praise JESUS (GOD) for His goodness and for His wonderful works He has shown to us.

## Dream Your Dream

Do not allow anyone to rob you or talk you out of your dream. Whether your dream is from your sleep or the dream of your mind, it will come through if you really want it bad enough. Muhammad Ali, the American professional boxer, activist, entertainer, poet, and philanthropist, nicknamed "The Greatest," could not be talked out of becoming the heavyweight champion. He said, "If you even dream of beating me, you'd better wake up and apologize. I am the greatest. I said that even before I knew I was. He who is not courageous enough to take risk will accomplish nothing in life." He also said, "Last night I had a dream, when I went to Africa, I had one hell of a rumble. I had to beat Tarzan behind first, for claiming to be king of the jungle." You can get it if really want it. All you have to do is try and try, and you will succeed.

If you believe in yourself and you are not afraid of meeting challenges, you shall have what you say. It is because of the lack of faith that we give up and blame someone or something. You should guard your thoughts against greed, for a man's life consist not in the abundance of the things that he possesses.

> JESUS spake a parable unto them, saying, "The ground of a certain rich man brought forth plentifully: and he thought within himself, saying, 'What shall I do, because I have no room to store my fruits?' And he said, 'This is what I will do; I will pull down my barns, and build greater ones. There I will store all fruit and my goods. I will say to my soul, "Soul, thou has much goods laid up for many years; take thy ease, eat, drink, and be merry." But GOD said unto him, 'Thou fool, this night your life will be demanded of you; and the things you have prepared, to whom will they belong?' So is he that store up treasure for himself, and is not rich toward GOD."

## Dream like Joseph

Now Joseph had a dream, and when he told it to his brothers, they hated him even more. He said to them, "Hear this dream that I have dreamed, my sheaf arose and stood upright. And behold, your sheaves gathered around it and bow down to my sheaf." His brothers said to him, "Are you indeed to reign over us?"

Then he dreamed another dream and told his brothers and said, "Behold, I have dreamed another. Behold, the sun, the moon, and the eleven stars were bowing down to me." But when he told his father and his brothers, his father rebuked him and said to him, "What is this dream that you have dreamed? Shall I and your mother and your brothers indeed come to bow down ourselves to the ground before you?" And his brothers were jealous of him, but his father kept the saying in mind.

Now his brothers went to pasture their father's flock near Shechem. And Israel said to Joseph, "Are not your brothers pasturing the flock at Shechem? Come, I will send you to them."

And he said, "Here I am."

"Go then," he replied. "See if all is well with your brothers and the flocks, and bring me words."

So he sent him off from the valley of Hebron. When Joseph reached Shechem, a man came upon him as he was wandering in the fields. "What are you looking for?" The man asked him.

"I am looking for my brothers," he answered. "Please tell me where they are tending the flocks."

The man told him, "They have moved on from here. Fact, I heard them say, 'Let us go to Dothan.'"

So Joseph went after his brothers and found them in Dothan. They saw him a distance, and before he reached them, they plotted to kill him. They said one to another, "Here comes that dreamer! Come now, let us kill him and then throw him into one of the cistern here. We could say a wild beast devoured him. We will see then what comes of his dreams."

Some Midianites merchantmen were passing by, so they sold him for twenty pieces of silver to the merchantmen, and did not take his life.

Joseph was brought into Egypt, and Midianites sold him to an officer of Pharaoh's guard, named Potiphar, a captain. So Joseph was in his master's house, and everything he did the LORD allowed it to prosper. When Potiphar, the captain, saw that Joseph was a prosperous man and the LORD was with him and gave him success in everything he did, Joseph found favor in his eyes and served him. Potiphar made Joseph overseer in his house and in the field. The blessing of the LORD was upon the captain's house and the field. He did not concern himself with anything, except the food he ate, with Joseph in charge. But with your dream comes the test and trials.

## With your dream comes the test and trials

Joseph was very handsome and well-built. On one occasion, he was in the house for a little while, his master's wife put him to the test. "Come to bed with me," she said to him.

He refused and explained to her. "My master does not concern himself with anything in this house. Everything is under my control except you. In this house, no one is greater than me. How could I do such a wicked thing and sin against GOD?"

She pleaded with Joseph day after day, but he refused her advances. One day he went into the house to do his chores. None of the servants were there. She grabbed him by his coat and said, "Come to bed with me." He ran out of the house, leaving his coat in her hand.

She was very displeased with what he did. She called the men of her house and spoke unto them and showed them his coat. She lied, saying, "Look, this Hebrew has been brought in to make sport of us. He came in here to sleep with me, but I screamed. He left his coat and ran out the house." She kept the coat until her husband came home. She said to him, "This Hebrew slave you brought in came to make sport of me. But as soon as I screamed for help. He left his coat beside me and ran out the house."

Burning with anger with what he heard, his master took him and put him in prison, the place where the king kept his prisoners. But the LORD was with Joseph and showed him kindness and granted him favor in the eyes of the prison warden. So the warden put Joseph in charge of the prisoners, and all that he did, GOD made it successful.

Later, two officials of the king offended him. Then Pharaoh was angry with the butler and the baker and put them in custody in the captain's house where Joseph was confined. The captain of the guard assigned them to Joseph, and he attended unto them. After they had been in custody for a while, the both men had a dream. Each dream had a meaning to it. The next morning Joseph came in unto them, "Why are you so sad today?" he asked them.

"The both of us had dreams, and there's no one to interpret them," they said.

So Joseph said, "Do not interpretations belong to the Lord? Tell me your dreams."

The butler said, "In my dream, I saw a vine in front of me, and the vine had three branches. As soon as it budded, it blossomed, and its clusters ripened into grapes. Pharaoh's cup was in my hand, I took the grapes and squeezed them into it and put the cup into Pharaoh's hand."

"This is what it means," said Joseph to him. "The three branches are three days. In three days, Pharaoh will lift up your head and restore you to your position, and you will put Pharaoh's cup in his hand just as you did before. When everything works out for you, remember me and show me kindness. Mention my name to Pharaoh to get me out of this place. I was carried away by force from the land of the Hebrews, and even here I have done nothing to be put in this dungeon."

When the chief baker saw that the interpretation was good, he said, "I too had a dream. On my head were three baskets of bread. In the top basket were all kinds of baked goods for Pharaoh, but the birds were eating them out of the basket on my head."

"This is what the dream means," said Joseph. "The three baskets are three days. Within three days, Pharaoh will lift up your head and hang you on a tree, and the birds will eat away your flesh."

In three days, Pharaoh had a birthday, and he made a feast for all his officials. He lifted up the head of the butler and the baker in the presence of his officials. He restored the butler to his position as before, and he gave the cup into Pharaoh's hand. But he hanged the baker just as Joseph interpreted to them. The chief butler, however, didn't remember Joseph. He forgot about him.

Joseph was in prison for eleven years. And after two full years had passed, Pharaoh had a dream. He did not know that the best was yet to come, for only GOD knows the future. In Pharaoh's dream, he was standing by the Nile river. Out of the river came up seven cows, fat and sleek, and they fed among the reeds. Then seven more cows came out gaunt and ugly, and they fed on the fat cows, so Pharaoh woke up. He went back to sleep, and he dreamed seven heads of corn on one stalk, very healthy. Then he saw seven other heads of corn, thin and scorched by the east wind. The thin heads swallowed up the healthy heads. Pharaoh woke up from another dream.

In the morning Pharaoh's mind was troubled. He sent and called for his magicians and wise men of Egypt. They could not give him an answer. The butler said to the king, "I remember my faults today. You were angry with me and the baker, and you put us in the dungeon. We both dreamed a dream the same night, and each dream had a meaning to it. A young Hebrew was there by the name Joseph. He gave us the meaning of the dreams. Me, you restored to my position, and him, you hanged.

So Pharaoh sent for Joseph. He shaved and changed his clothes and came to him. Pharaoh said, "I hear that you can interpret a dream when you hear it."

"I can't do it," Joseph said to the king. "But GOD will give Pharaoh an answer of peace."

The king told Joseph the dreams.

And Joseph said to Pharaoh, "GOD is one, the dream is one. What GOD is about to do, He has showed thee. The reason the dream was doubled unto Pharaoh is because the thing is established by GOD, and He will bring it to pass soon. Seven years of plenty are coming throughout the land of Egypt, but seven years of famine will follow them. Then all the abundance in Egypt will be forgotten, and the famine will ravage the land."

Joseph continued, "Now let Pharaoh look for a discerning and wise man and put him over the land. They should collect all the food of these good years that are coming and store up the grain, under the authority of Pharaoh, to be in the cities for food. This food should be kept in reserve for the country, to be used during the seven years of famine that will come upon Egypt so that the country may not be ruined by the famine."

The plan seemed good to Pharaoh and all his officials. So Pharaoh asked them, "Can we find anyone like this man, one in whom is the spirit of GOD?" Then Pharaoh said to Joseph, "Since GOD has made known all this to you, I will put you in charge of my palace, and according to thy word shall all my people be ruled. Only in the throne will I be greater than thee." And Pharaoh said to Joseph, "See, I have set thee over all of Egypt."

Pharaoh took off the ring from his hand and put it on Joseph's hand and arrayed him in vestures of fine linen and put a gold chain about his neck, and he made him ride in the second chariot that he had. And they cried before him, "Bow the knee." Pharaoh reassured Joseph by saying, "I am Pharaoh, and without thee shall no man lift up his hand or foot in all the land of Egypt."

## Joseph's dreams and visions came to pass

Joseph went out from the presence of Pharaoh and went throughout all the land of Egypt with his wife, Asenath, whom the king gave him. He went to work as the governor of Egypt and did as he counseled Pharaoh.

The seven years of plenty came and ended. Joseph's wife, Asenath, had two sons for him, whom he named Manasseh and the, second, Ephraim. Joseph said, "Manasseh means GOD made me forget all my troubles and my father's household. Ephraim means GOD made me fruitful in the land of my suffering."

The famine came in the land just as Joseph had said, but in Egypt, there was food. When the Egyptians began to feel the famine, the people cried to Pharaoh for food. Pharaoh said to the people, "Go to Joseph, and whatever he tells you do it."

As the famine spreads, the world came to buy food in Egypt from Joseph, and he opened all the storehouses and sold food to them.

Jacob heard and saw that there was grain in Egypt. He said to his sons, "Don't just sit there looking at each other. Go down to Egypt and buy some food that we live and not die."

Then ten of Joseph's brothers went down to Egypt to buy food, except little Benjamin. Jacob was afraid that harm would come to him and didn't send him.

When Joseph's brothers arrived, they bowed down to him with their faces to the ground.

Joseph recognized his brothers and spoke to them harshly. "Where do you come from?"

"From the land of Canaan to buy food," they replied.

Joseph remembered his dreams about them and said to them, "You have come as spies to see where the land is unprotected."

They answered Joseph, "No, my lord, your servants are not spies. We are all sons of one man. We are honest."

"You have come to see where our land is unprotected," Joseph said again.

They replied, "Your servants were twelve brothers, the sons of one man who lives in Canaan. The youngest is now with our father, and one is no more."

## Testing time again

Joseph said to his brothers, who did not recognize him, "As sure as Pharaoh lives, you will not leave this place unless your youngest brother comes here. Decide who will go for your brother? The rest of you will remain here in prison until he comes to prove you are not spies, for I fear GOD."

Joseph spoke to his brothers with the help of an interpreter. He listened as they said one to another, "We are guilty concerning our brother, in that we saw the pain on his face, when he begged us and we would not hear. Therefore, this evil is come upon us."

Reuben replied, "I said to you at that time, don't sin against the child. You would not hear. Therefore, his blood is required at our hands."

As they blamed each other, Joseph turned aside and wept. He returned to them and communed with them. He took Simeon and bound him before their eyes. He had placed them in prison for three days. Joseph commanded to fill their sacks with corn and restore every man's money into his sack and give them provision for the way. While on their way home, they stopped to feed the asses and opened their sack. They were shocked to find the money they had brought to purchase their goods. They were afraid and said, "What is this GOD has done unto us?"

## The report

The brothers came home and told their father, Jacob, all that they went through how they found the money in their sacks after leaving the place of their confines. They told Jacob that the man wants to see their youngest brother.

Jacob said, "Joseph is not here. Simeon is not here. My son will not go down with you. If mischief befall him by the way you go, I will go to my grave with gray hairs sorrowful."

The famine was so severe. They had eaten all the corn that they brought out of Egypt. Jacob said, "Go again to Egypt and buy us a little food."

Judah said, "Dad, the man said to us, 'If you don't bring your brother, you will not see my face.' We will not go without Benjamin.'"

Jacob said, "If it must be so now, do this. Take some of the best fruits, a little balm, a little honey, spices, myrrh, nuts and almonds as a present for the man. Take extra money in your hand, with the money you found in your sacks. It might be an oversight. Take your brother also and go to the man. GOD Almighty gives you mercy before the man, that he may let your brother and Benjamin come back with you. As for me, if I am bereaved, I am bereaved."

When they came to Egypt and Joseph saw Benjamin with them, he told the steward of his house, "Take these men to my house, slaughter an animal and prepare a meal. They are to eat with me at noon."

When they got to Joseph's house, they thought it was because of the money they found in their sacks, and they were afraid. They made confessions to the steward about their ordeal, and they said to him, "We brought additional money to buy food. We don't know who put back the silver in our sack."

"It's all right," said the steward. "Don't be afraid. Your GOD, the GOD of your father, has given you treasure in your sacks. I had your money." And he brought Simeon out to them. They did not realize that their best was yet to come.

*Your GOD, the GOD of your father, has given you treasure in your sacks*

When Joseph came home, they presented him the gifts they brought into the house and bowed down to the ground before him.

Joseph asked them, "How are you doing today? How is your aged father you told me about? Is he still living?"

They replied, "Your servant, our father, is still alive and well." And again, they bowed down, prostrating themselves before him.

He looked; and Benjamin, his mother's son, was there. Joseph said to them. "Is this your little brother you told me about?" He also said, "GOD be gracious to you, my son."

He was deeply moved at the sight of his brother. Joseph hurried out into his private room to weep. He washed his face, came out, and controlled himself.

Food was served to the brothers by themselves. Benjamin sat by himself, and his food was five times more than his brothers. Joseph sat by himself in the same dining area and his brothers, for to eat with the Egyptians is a sin.

Joseph told the steward, "Give them as much food as they can carry. Put each man's in the mouth of his sack. Then put my silver cup in the young boy's sack along with the money for the grain."

And he did so.

As daylight came, the men were sent on their way. They had not gone far from the city when Joseph said to the steward, "Go after those men now. Say to them, 'Why have you repaid evil for good? Is not this the cup which my lord drinks from, and whereby he divines? This is a wicked thing you have done.'"

He caught up with them and repeated what Joseph said.

But they denied it, saying, "Why does my lord say such things? We brought to you the money we found in our luggage when we came. Search! Whomsoever has it will die. The rest of us will be your servants."

"Very well, I take you at your words," he said.

They all lowered their sacks and opened them. The steward searched the eldest brother and ended with the youngest. Behold the cup was in Benjamin's sack. They tore their clothes, reloaded their asses, and returned to the city.

Judah and his brothers came into the house, and Joseph was there. They threw themselves before him on the ground. And Joseph said to them, "What have you done? Don't you know that a man like me can find things out?"

Judah said, "What can I say to my lord? GOD has uncovered your servant's guilt. We are all your servants."

Joseph said, "GOD forbids that I should do such a thing. The one with the cup will be my slave. The rest of you will go in peace to your father."

Judah went close to Joseph and said, "Don't be angry with your servant, although you are equal to Pharaoh himself. Remember you asked us about our father and we told you everything. We have one father. One of his sons is dead, and the little boy that he loves, we brought him here, because you said so. I pray thee let me be your slave and let the boy return with his brothers, for I promised my father his safety. How can I go back to my father if the boy is not with me? Do not let me see my father's misery."

## Surprise! Surprise!

After Joseph heard Judah's plea for mercy, he cried out, "All the Egyptians go out from me." He started weeping loudly. The Egyptians and the house of Pharaoh heard him. Joseph said to his brothers, "I am Joseph. Is my father still living?"

They did not respond, for they were surprised at the saying. So he said to them again, "Come close to me." They did so!

"I am your brother Joseph, the one you sold into Egypt. Don't be angry and distressed with yourselves for selling me here. It was for saving your lives GOD sent me ahead of you, to do so with a great deliverance. GOD sent me here. It was not you. He made me a father to Pharaoh, lord to his entire household, and ruler over all Egypt. Go quickly and tell my father of all my glory you have seen and the eyes of my brother Benjamin have seen." He kissed Benjamin, his brother, and cried. Then he kissed the others and cried.

Pharaoh, the king, was happy when he heard of Joseph's father and his brothers. He told Joseph, "Tell your brothers to go get your father and his household and come. I will give you the good of the land to enjoy. Take some wagons from here for your children, your wives, and get your father and come. Don't worry about your stuff. The best of Egypt is yours."

Joseph blessed his brethren immensely and gave Benjamin three hundred pieces of silver and five suits of clothing and sent them away. As they were leaving, Joseph said to his brothers, "Don't quarrel on the way."

They came home with excitement and told their father, "Joseph is alive! He is ruler over Egypt."

Jacob was stunned. He did not believe them. So they told him what Joseph said, and when he saw the wagons, his spirit revived. Jacob said, "I am convinced! My son is still alive. I will go and see him before I die." Jacob was patient and positive at the same time, knowing that his best was yet to come. GOD's word gives assurance when you enlarge your dreams and visions in Him.

### Did you do it? Enlarge your vision?

Jacob, who is Israel, set out on his journey with all that was his. When he reached Beersheba, he offered sacrifices to the GOD of his father Isaac. That night, while Jacob slept, the LORD GOD spoke to him in a vision and gave him assurance.

"I am God, the God of your father. Don't fear to go down into Egypt. I will go down with you and bring you back. I will make you a great nation. Joseph's own hand will close your eyes."

Joseph made ready his chariot and went to meet his father in Goshen. As soon as Joseph saw his father, he threw his arms around him and wept for a long time.

Jacob said to Joseph, "Now I am ready to die since I have seen for myself that you are still alive."

Jacob lived in Goshen for seventeen years, and then he died. Joseph went and buried his father.

After the burial of his father, Joseph returned to Egypt with his brothers and the others who went to the burial.

When Joseph's brothers saw that their father was dead, they said, "What if Joseph holds a grudge against us and pay us back for all the wrong we did to him?" So they sent and told Joseph, "This is what your father said before he died: 'I am asking you to forgive your brothers sins and the wrongs they committed in treating you so badly.'" So they said, "Please forgive the sins of the God of your father."

When the messenger told Joseph, he wept.

The brothers then came and threw themselves down before him and said, "We are your servants."

But Joseph said to them, "Don't be afraid. Am I in the place of God? But as for you, your intent was to harm me, but God intended it for good to accomplish what's now being done, to save much people alive. Don't be afraid. I will provide for you and you children." Joseph reassured them and spoke kindly to them about his God who came to His own people.

## Don't Hold a Grudge

> Do not grudge against one another, brethren, lest you be condemned. Behold the Judge is standing at the door. (James 5:9)

You can be healed if you will let go of your grudge. Letting go creates growth. When you let go of resentment, you can open your heart to others. You will see yourself as a winner and not a victim. Your responsibility should not be diminished in giving to another person. Just try your best not to mistreat anyone. Letting go the grudge frees you from the pain. You may try to justify yourself in grudging, but it will not benefit you.

In order not to be condemned yourself, you must forgive. "If you will not forgive men of their trespass, you will not be forgiven of yours." It is possible to be redeemed. I will try my best to help you to make your life better. Holding a grudge will land me and keep me in the devil's territory.

To prove yourself right, you must release the urge at all times. If you keep holding to the negative, you will never let go of your grudge. If you want to live a life of joy and gratitude, get rid of your negativity. Letting go of a grudge is not hard. You can make your life more difficult by holding on to your grudge.

When Joseph's brothers said, "What if Joseph holds a grudge against us and pays us back for the wrong we did to him?" this is because they were being killed by their own conscience. But Joseph said plainly, "I fear GOD. Don't you be afraid. I will provide for you and your children."

> Therefore, as GOD's chosen people, holy and dearly loved, clothe yourself with compassion, kindness, humility, gentleness and patience. Bear with each other, and forgiving one another; if any man have a quarrel against any, forgive as the LORD forgave you. (Col. 3:12 NIV)

> Perfect love cast out fear. (1 John 4:18)

GOD has blessings that will thrust you years ahead. Often, these blessings overtake us, if we strive to please the LORD. Most, I believe, would love to see their blessings ahead of them and reach for them. The blessings of the LORD make you rich, and there are no sorrows to it. The LORD laid up the blessings of the sinners for the righteous. They that trust in their GOD shall not want any good thing. If you trust in the LORD and patiently wait for Him and on Him, He will bring forth your blessing. You don't have to worry about doing evil. GOD will show you great and mighty things that you know not. Joseph said to his brothers,

> I am Joseph. Come near to me, I pray you. I am Joseph whom you sold into Egypt. Now therefore be not grieved, nor angry with yourselves that you sold me here, because it was to save lives that GOD sent me ahead of you.
>
> For two years now, there has been famine in the land, and for the next five years, there will be no plowing and reaping. But GOD sent me ahead of you to preserve for you a remnant on the earth and to save your lives by a great deliverance. So then, it was not you who sent me here, but GOD. He made me a father to Pharaoh, lord of his entire household, and ruler of all Egypt.
>
> Now hurry back and say to my father this is what your son, Joseph says, "GOD has made me lord over all Egypt. Come down to me, tarry not. You shall live in the region of Goshen land be near me, you, your grandchildren, your flocks and herds, and all that you have. I will provide for you there, because five years of famine are still to come; lest you and your household, and all you have come to poverty." (Gen. 45:3–11)

In 1991, George, an ex-coworker of mine, was hospitalized in Takoma Park, Maryland, with a deadly body tissue called gangrene. One Sunday, on the way from worship, my wife, Amy, and I went to visit him. When we went into his room, his right leg was in a stirrup. The leg was swollen from his groin to his toes. He told us how the doctors said his condition was very bleak. They will have to amputate his leg at the groin. He would not be able to have children, nor return to work. The leg was green in color and swollen too.

Overtaken with empathy, I asked him, "Do you believe GOD can heal you?"

He said, "Yes, Mr. J. I do believe. Do you remember back in 1988 when I had the migraine headache and I asked you to pray for me and the LORD healed me? Please to pray for me again."

So I read James 5:14–20, prayed for him, and anointed him with oil in the name of JESUS CHRIST.

While I was reading the Word, a man, who is Jewish and was behind the other curtain, pulled it aside and said, "Can you pray for me too?"

I asked him the same question: "Do you believe that GOD can heal you?"

He said, "Yes."

I prayed for him and said goodbye to both of them.

The next day, Monday, I went back to the hospital with some food my wife had promised George. While there, I anointed both feet with oil in the name of JESUS CHRIST and said goodbye.

At 1:15 p.m. the following day, Tuesday, I called the hospital and asked for my call to be transferred to his room. The young lady did. The phone rang several times without an answer. The young lady that answered in the beginning said, "Sir, no one is answering."

I said to her, "Madam, I came there on Monday, and George was there."

She said, "Just one moment." A few minutes later, she said, "Sir, he was discharged yesterday."

I picked up my phone and called George. The phone rang. No answer. At 4:30 p.m., I called back, and George answered with excitement. He said, "Mr. J, Mr. J, GOD healed me. I am okay. It's just a little tender, but I'm okay."

I asked him about the other man whom I prayed for, and he said, "He was discharged too."

This man that the doctors gave discouraging words was healed, returned to work as a baker, and had a child, a boy, with his wife. After this miracle from GOD, I spoke to him again the Word. He and his wife were baptized by me in the mighty saving name of JESUS CHRIST.

"Oh, the depths of the riches and wisdom and knowledge of GOD! How unsearchable are His judgments and decisions and how unfathomable and untraceable are His ways." "Who forgives all thine iniquities, and who heals all thy diseases."

## My Declaration

I declare GOD will accelerate His plans for my life and yours as we put our trust in Him. We can accomplish our dreams faster than we thought possible. It will not take years to overcome an obstacle, to get out of debt, or to meet the right person. The LORD GOD is doing things faster than before. He will give us the victory sooner than we think.

> Blessed be the GOD and Father, our LORD JESUS CHRIST, who has blessed us with all spiritual blessings in heavenly places in CHRIST. For He choose us in Him before the creation of the world to be holy and blameless in His sight in love. He predestinated us for adoption by JESUS CHRIST to Himself, in accordance with His pleasure and will. In whom also we have obtained an inheritance after the counsel of His own will. (Eph. 1:3–5)

> If you fully obey the LORD your GOD and carefully follow all His commands, I give you this day, the LORD your GOD will set you high above all nations on earth. All these blessings will come on you and overtake you, if you obey the LORD your GOD. You will be blessed in the city and in the field. The fruit of your womb will be blessed, and the crops of your land, the young of your livestock calves of your herds, and the lambs of

your flocks. Blessed shall be thy basket and thy
store. You will be blessed when you come in, and
blessed when you go out. (Deut. 28:1–6)

The man that trusts in the LORD is blessed. The woman that
trusts in the LORD is blessed. The boy and girl that trust in the LORD
are blessed and all who hopes in Him. In Him, we have redemption
through His blood, even the forgiveness of sins. JESUS CHRIST is our
vine; we are branches in Him if we abide by the Word. If we do, we
will produce a lot, for apart from Him, we can do nothing. Everyone
will walk in the name of his god, but if we trust in the LORD with all
our heart, He has blessings that will thrust us years ahead. But you
have to be honest with yourself and maybe invite a friend and go to
the house of the LORD, He has honest men that will teach you of His
ways. He has honest women that will teach other women the truth
about honoring GOD in prayer by covering your head.

You will be able to discern between the righteous and those
who are wicked, between the one that serves GOD honestly. You shall
feed in the blessings of the LORD, in the majesty of His name, for He
is our peace. He has blessings that will thrust you years ahead. Our
GOD is a disciplined Man, for He brought the people out of Egypt
and redeemed them out of the house of bondage servants. He sent
before them Moses, Aaron, and Miriam as leaders. The LORD blessed
His people, and he who blesses you will be blessed and those that
curse you are cursed themselves. Just remember what Balak, the king
of Moab, did. He consulted the man of GOD, Balaam, to curse the
people and the answer he finally gave to the king to know the righteousness of the LORD. Don't you fear. It's GOD's will to give you His
kingdom. So give to those who are in need, even if you have to sell
your goods, bonds, house, land, and stocks. Give and He will give to
you. GOD's Word gives you assurance: the more you give, the more
He gives to you. If you look into the perfect Word (law) that sets you
free, if you do what it says and don't forget what you have read, the
LORD GOD will bless you for doing it and thrust you ahead.

If you're healthy and are able to move about on your own, it's
a blessing that will thrust you ahead. And even if you are sick to the

point of death and can't move, it's not over until GOD said it's over. It's not over until GOD says it's the end. Is there not an appointed time for you upon the earth? You are made to possess months and years of vanity and wearisome nights. You lie down and say, "I wonder when will I arise?" You go to sleep. You toss and turn until the day dawns. In the morning you rise, and in the anguish of your spirit, you complain in the bitterness of your thoughts (soul), "Maybe it's better for me to die than to live."

If you have not been reconciled to GOD, be honest enough to go down on your knees and say to GOD, "I have sinned. Oh, thou preserver of men, preserve me. Why has thou set me as a mark against myself? Please to pardon me and take away my transgression. Take away my iniquities from me. If not, I will sleep in the dust of the earth and be no more." Seek the Almighty often and make supplication to Him saying, "My soul is weary of my life. I will not be angry with you LORD. Please remember that thou has made me fashioned me together round about. You made me out of clay. Please don't allow the enemy to take my life. Woe to me if I am wicked, and yet I will not lift up my head to boast that I am righteous, for I'm full of confusion from day to day without GOD."

In the days of King Hezekiah's reign, he became ill to the point of death. The prophet Isaiah, the son of Amoz, went to him and said, "This is what the LORD says: 'Put your house in order, because you are going to die; you will not recover.'" Hezekiah turned his face to the wall and prayed to the LORD, "Remember, LORD, how I have walked before you faithfully and with a perfect heart, and have done what is good in your eyes." And he wept bitterly.

Then the Word of the LORD came to Isaiah: "Go and tell Hezekiah this is what the LORD, the GOD of your father David, says, 'I have heard your prayer and seen your tears. I will add fifteen years to your life. And I will deliver you and this city from the hand of the king of Assyria. I will defend this city. This is the LORD's sign to you that the LORD will do what He has promised: I will make the shadow cast by the sun go back the ten degrees (steps) it has gone down on the stairway of Ahaz.'" So the sun went backward the ten degrees (steps) it had gone down. Isaiah had told Hezekiah to take a lump of figs, beat it into a soft moist mass (poultice), and keep it in place with a bandage or cloth and he will recover.

After the recovery, Hezekiah said,

> What can I say? The LORD has spoken to me, and He Himself has done this. I will walk humbly all my years because of the anguish of my soul. It is good to be humble and obedient. LORD, by such things people live and my spirit finds life in them too. You restored my health and make me live. Surely it was for my benefit that I suffered such anguish. In your love You have kept me from the pit of destruction; you have put all my sins behind your back. For the grave cannot praise you, death cannot sing your praise; those who go down to the pit cannot hope for your faithfulness. The living, the living, they shall praise you, as I am doing today; parents tell their children about Your faithfulness, saying, "The LORD will save me, and we will sing with stringed instruments all the days of our lives in the house(temple) of the LORD." (Isa. 38)

GOD's blessings thrust Hezekiah fifteen years ahead.

## Do You Really Know That You Are Blessed

Has thou not heard? Has thou not known? The LORD will come to rescue with strong hands, and His arms shall rule for Him. He carries His reward with Him. He will feed you as a shepherd feeds his flock. He will gather you in His arms and carry you in His bosom. You are so faint, perplexed, weary, sad, and worn out. Yet with your faith in the LORD, He gives you blessings and power that will thrust you years ahead. The LORD will help you. He will not cast you away. He will uphold you with His righteousness. He will always do a new thing for you. The LORD has openly shown you His righteousness. He has not dealt with you as your deeds and wrong deserves.

You should be praising the LORD GOD. Do you really know that you are blessed? Wealth and riches will be in your house, for the LORD has been mindful of you. So when they closed the doors in your face, don't give in and don't give up. He has a door opened and waiting for you to enter. You are blessed. Just walk in the door and be a blessing to someone else. You are so faithless. You just can't see that things are not as bad as you make it out to be. The door is open. You receive the job you need, but instead of being grateful and thankful, you start complaining. But before you received the job, you knew very well what the payment and benefits were. You are blessed with a job. You should please your boss well, showing good fidelity. You were hired and paid according to your ability. Be grateful and be thankful. You are blessed.

You are blessed. Be a team player, not a complainer. You are blessed to be a blessing; so do your work without complaining, disputing, and murmuring. The LORD blesses us according to our several abilities. How great is GOD's blessing that He has laid up for you that fear Him the things He bestow in the sight of all on those who take refuge in Him. All the people that you know in your lifetime who are rich or wealthy or those whom you have read about only enjoy so much of them. When they came into the world, they brought nothing, so enjoy the blessings of GOD that He has given.

Whether you are working or not working, poor or rich, and you are content with what GOD has given you is great gain. But your greatest gain is to seek the LORD while He may be found. Call on Him while He is near. Forsake your way and your unrighteous thoughts. Choose GOD's way in which the righteous must walk. Although you have or have had many sins, He will wash them all away and abundantly pardon you. You will go out with joy and be led with the peace of GOD that passes all human understanding.

GOD the Almighty came to His own people to give them blessings that will thrust them years ahead. But His own people received Him not. They were not interested in the blessings He offered them. Those that received Him, to them He gave power to become sons of

GOD and thrust you years ahead, as many of you who believe in His name. We easily believe the men's witness, but JESUS *says*, "Whoever believes and is baptized in water in My name (JESUS CHRIST), your sins shall be removed, and you shall receive the gift of the HOLY SPIRIT, the promise He made unto you, your children, and to all who are far off."

Believe in your GOD. He will save you and establish you.

> Blessed are the poor in spirit, for theirs the kingdom of heaven. Blessed are they that mourn, for they shall be comforted. Blessed are the meek, they shall inherit the earth. Blessed are they which do hunger and thirst after righteousness, for they shall be filled. Blessed are the merciful for they shall obtain mercy. Blessed are the pure in heart, for they shall see GOD. Blessed are the peace makers, for they shall be called the children of GOD. Blessed are they which are persecuted for righteousness sake, for theirs the kingdom of heaven. Blessed are you, when men shall revile you, and shall say all manner of evil against you falsely, for My sake; rejoice, and be exceedingly glad for great is your reward in heaven, for so they persecuted the prophets which were before you. (Matt. 5:3–12)

Just remember, the LORD will make you the head and not the tail. Believe that you are the head, and keep tight security on the gate of your mind, that only positive thoughts are allowed to enter and only words of wisdom are allowed to get out. With GOD, you future will always be better than your past. Just remember to surround yourself with people who will encourage you and are happy to see you. Succeed in every way possible. Anything that hurt you, move on, and what it taught you, never forget. If and when you fail, it does not mean you are struggling. Every great success requires some worthy type of struggle to get you where you want to be. Things that are good will take you some time. Be positive and patient at the same time. Eventually, everything will come through for you, maybe not immediately but soon.

As you read this book today, remember you are created to succeed. You are designed to win. You are equipped to overcome. You are anointed to prosper and blessed to be a blessing. My friend, you have the awesome ability to make a difference in someone's life. Strive hard and just do it. Be fair, be honest, be kind, and be truthful—all these things will come back to you in a jiffy. For the eyes of the LORD run to and fro throughout the whole earth, showing Himself strong on behalf of those whose heart is perfect toward Him. The LORD will surely bring you out of your troubles if you put your confidence and trust in Him. He has the blessings that will thrust you years ahead.

## Lord, You Are My Judge

On March 3, 2017, my GOD inspired me; and I sat down and begin to write these words:

Judge me, O LORD my GOD according to thy righteousness. Let no one rejoice over me. LORD, You plead my case with them that strive with me. You, LORD, fight against them that fight against me. Let them be ashamed and brought to confusion together that rejoice at my hurt. Let them be clothed with shame and dishonor that magnify themselves against me. Let them not say in their hearts, "Ah, so will we have our desire." Let them not say, we have swallowed him up. Let them be confounded and put to shame that seek after my soul. Please let them be turned back and brought to confusion that devise my hurt. Let them be as the dust and the leaves before the wind, and let the angel of the LORD chase them. Oh, loving Savior, tender and true, let their way be dark and slippery. And let the angel of the LORD persecute them. For only You, LORD, know that without cause, they hid a net in a pit for me, which without cause they have dug for my soul.

Oh, how You cares for my soul. Let destruction come upon them unawares, and into that very destructive pit, let them fall. For only You alone knows, LORD, that false witnesses did rise up against me. They laid to my charge things I knew not. Surely, I have been rewarded evil for doing good. But I commit my way to You, LORD. I am trusting in You and doing good, and you are feeding me. I delight myself in you.

I know without a doubt the LORD, my GOD, is giving me the desires of my heart. Let me not be ashamed, O LORD, for I am calling on Thee. Let the wicked be silent, and let them be ashamed. Let the lying lips be put to silence that speak grievous things proudly and contemptuously against me. While they were lurking in their dark places and taking counsel together against me, the enemy brought fear upon me from every side. They devised to take away my life, for I had heard the slander of many of them, and I became a reproach among all my enemies, especially among my neighbors. But I trust in Thee, oh LORD. I said, Thou art my GOD. My times are in Your hand. Deliver me from the hands of my enemies and from them that persecute me. I will be glad and rejoice in Thy mercy, for Thou has considered my trouble. I became a little recalcitrant and in my haste, I said, "I am cut off from before Thee." Nevertheless, Thou LORD heard the voice of my supplications when I cry unto Thee.

LORD, pull me out of the net that they have laid privately for me. My LORD, my GOD, I commit myself in Thine hands. Many are my afflictions, oh LORD, but You deliver me out of them all. The wicked plotted against me. They took one of my client's tax return and amended it (do over). They went to my client's place of residence and waited in the hallway. They flashed their badges to the client and said, "I am special agent C. W. May we come in?"

My client said, "No, you may not. And what is this all about? Whatever it is, we are staying right here in the hallway."

The agent presented a document to the client and said, "This is your tax return. Mr. Williams did it over."

My client retorted, "No, you are lying. Mr. Williams did not do that. Before I went to Mr. Williams, I had something like that done at my previous taxman, but not Mr. Williams. By the way, I am going to tell Mr. Williams. He did not do that. You did that."

The agent responded, "Please don't tell him."

My client said, "Goodbye, I am going to tell Mr. Williams."

The wicked throw out their words. Their tongue is as a bow and arrow against a poor man like me to slay me. The LORD is laughing at them, for He sees that their day is coming. Their words against me shall enter into their own hearts, and they shall be broken. Oh LORD, my GOD, in thee do I put my trust deliver me from them that persecute me and save me. LORD, You are my defense. LORD, You are my Judge and my wonderful Counselor. Behold, the LORD will help me. Who is he that shall condemn me? When I pray, I received the law from Your mouth and lay up Your Word in my heart.

Yes, the Almighty is my defense and jury. I will wait on the LORD and be of good courage. He will strengthen my heart. Yes! He will. The LORD, my GOD, has given me the blessings He promised to Abraham, Isaac, and Jacob. Thank you, LORD, for my prison experience of knowledge, and understanding, and wisdom. My GOD has given me test, trials, and tribulation. And as time progresses, my family come to me, saying, "Why did you really go to prison? What does it all mean?" Then I shall say, "I was held as the United States bondsman in commerce and the confiscation of my credit, and the LORD brought me to Butner Prison Camp to teach me and bring me out and delivered me, to bring me in to give me the land and all the blessings He swore to our fathers to give them."

The LORD did not set His love upon me nor choose me, little me versus the Unites States than anyone else because I was good, but because the LORD loves me. He is keeping the oath He had sworn to our fathers Abraham, Isaac, and Jacob. He brought me here to Butner to redeem me out of the hands of the US BOP.

## Blessed Be the Lord

Had it not been for the LORD who was on my side, when men rose up against me, they would have swallowed me up quick when their wrath was kindled against me. Blessed be the LORD, who has not given me as a prey to their teeth. Their hearts are like an oven. Their sins engulf them. They practice deceit, but they do not realize that the LORD remembers all their evil deeds. GOD wants to redeem them, but they speak about Him falsely. They do not cry out to GOD from their hearts. They boast upon their beds; and when things go wrong, they use their laws, lies, and their money as their defense.

Because the wicked are so proud, they talked up a storm for destruction and will not seek GOD for help.

But why did they persecute me, seeing the root of the problem is found in them? Why do the wicked live long and become old and mighty in power? They spent their days in their wealth and say unto GOD, "Depart from us. We do not desire the knowledge of Your ways." They say faith doesn't work in courtroom. Who is GOD that we should serve Him? Will there be a profit if we pray unto Him? But while they were judging me, my GOD was judging them. For the LORD knows their thoughts and the devices that they have wrongfully imagined against me.

Blessed be GOD who has reserved the wicked for the day of destruction. They will be paid for what they did to me. GOD performs the things that He has appointed me, and many such things are with Him. My GOD, who called me to His glory in JESUS CHRIST, allows me to go through some suffering for a while. He will Himself restore me and make me strong, firm, and steadfast, abounding in the work of the LORD.

## Praise the Lord

The LORD heard my supplications and my voice because He has inclined His ears unto me. He has been mindful of me and never leaves me alone. I really love the LORD. You don't know what He has done for me. Let me tell you. He has given me the victory. And I praised Him every day with my songs and my voice, and every time I get a chance to play the guitar, I praise GOD. The LORD is worthy of all my praise. I am not troubled or worried about what man is doing unto me. I asked the LORD to make me live and deal with me bountifully, so I keep His Word.

I kept singing this song:

> I was guilty of all the charges; but JESUS, with
> His special love, reached down with His arms so
> strong. He picked me up, turned me around,

JULIUS WILLIAMS

gave me a brand-new song. JESUS dropped the charges. Now I'm saved through faith and grace.

I asked the LORD to let more of His mercies come unto me and take not the Word of truth out of my mouth, for He is closer than a brother to me. He's my dearest friend, in everything I need. He is my hiding place, my rock, and my shield. He pleads my cause and deliver me. Blessed be the LORD Who has not given me as a prey to the hyena's teeth when they rise against me. The LORD has done great things for me and has perfected the things concerning me.

I have been brought very, very low. Deliver me from my persecutors who are stronger than me. I said unto the LORD, "You are my GOD. I will ever love and trust You, and in Your presence, daily I live." I remember the old rugged cross on which my LORD was crucified, for such death was needed to save my soul from death. JESUS is the true foundation. He's the LORD and King of all. I will ever love and trust him, and in His presence, daily I live. I know my LORD is coming back again to this old world for His own, and I'll be going up to heaven with Him, for I have the love and power of JESUS in my heart.

JESUS is my Savior, a precious friend to me. There was once a time that my heart was condemned to die. JESUS paid the ransom for me. I bid this world goodbye, and now that JESUS wants me, I will be ready to die. For if I miss heaven, all my hope in this world will be doomed. It would be better if I weren't born for what would I say to GOD when I meet Him at the judgment throne. I would be so confused if I'm refused when the roll is called, in hell, I will lift up my eyes. So, LORD, please hear my cry and don't let my soul go to hell to die.

I have confidence that GOD will see me through, no matter what the case may be. I know He will fix it for me. As I wake up this morning, I truly have no doubt that, You LORD, will drop the charges, remove the restitution, and give me the victory. Thank You, LORD, for Your many blessings on me. Once you trust GOD and never doubt, He will surely bring you out. You have to believe in yourself that all things are possible through JESUS CHRIST. The LORD

100

is well pleased with His righteousness. He magnifies His Word. It will not return to Him void.

GOD's people are robbed and snared. They all are accused before Him daily. Some of them are hid in prison houses. They are hidden as a prey and for spoil. When you find yourself in a position like this, who can deliver you and restore your losses but GOD? Who among you will give ear to this? Who will hearken for the time to come? For you have need of some patience, knowing that GOD made you a promise to be with you in trouble and when things are rough and tough. Do not throw away your confidence that you are holding to in JESUS. Just remember what He said: He that will come, will come. He will not linger. The believer must live by faith in JESUS CHRIST. His Word gives assurance: He will never leave you nor will He forsake you.

# I HAVE THE VICTORY, SO CAN YOU

## My Prison Journey and Experience

After the judge had sentenced me and told the marshal "to get this man," I was taken back to Charles County Detention Center. I was kept there for three weeks and then taken to Baltimore, Maryland, where I remained for one week. From there we were bused to Pittsburg, Pennsylvania. There they put us on a plane, and we ended up in Oklahoma City, where we spent the night. After we have had about one hour and fifteen minutes sleep, we were awaken and given a quick snack. The officers put us on a bus, drove us around the city, picking up prisoners from halfway houses. We were taken to a large landing strip, where the officers loaded us into a huge green-ish-in-color plane. After some hours of flight, the plane landed. We were now in Ossining, New York. From there, they flew us back to Pittsburg, Pennsylvania. And there, they placed us in three buses and took us to Morgan Town, West Virginia.

When we arrived in Morgantown prison camp for checking in, my medical record, which was with the officers, could not be found. And according to intake, there was no medical information in the computer system about me. My medical problems were high blood pressure, an enlarged prostate, and lower back pain and tingling that radiated down in both feet. That very night they gave me medication for blood pressure and prostate pain. At 5:00 a.m. just before daylight, I went to use the urinal and thought I was back lying down on my bunk.

I was taken to the Ruby Memorial Hospital, Morgantown. About six hours later, while sleeping, I felt a touched and someone calling, "Mr. Williams, I am your doctor. Do you know where you are?"

I opened my eyes and replied, "Good morning, Doctor. I am on my bunk."

He said, "No, you are in the hospital. You are pretty banged up. You received five stiches on the top of your head. We will do everything to make you well."

After staying there for four days, I was released and given a prescription: Lisinopril 40mg, with some instructions to take with me back to the camp, which I did. The prescription was never filled. But the medical team at the Morgantown prison camp kept giving me their own recommended medication and dosage, which made me sick and cause me to faint four other times and seeing the place spinning out of control. I had to be placed in a wheelchair for three months and then given a sitting walker to help with my mobility.

On February 9, 2016, I woke up feeling weak in my chest and my stomach. I went to the medical unit for assistance, and I was the second person in line to go in the building. There were twenty men in all that needed medical attention. I sat there from 6:45 a.m. until 10:15 a.m. The nurse called the last prisoner before me. I heard him say to the nurse, "This man has been here before and waiting a long time. He is lying down and sweating profusely." At that moment, they came quickly and helped me up. They carried me to a room and hooked me up to a machine. The nurse cried out, "Oh my GOD, his heart stopped beating."

They called the ambulance, which came in a flash. They put me in the ambulance and hooked me up and administered some medicine and kept talking to me until we got to the hospital. Although my heart was not beating, my eyes were open, and I could hear them, for GOD's mercy kept me alive, and I did not give up the ghost. When I got to the emergency room, twelve doctors came and surrounded me. I was quickly rushed to a room where they inserted a small tube in my left arm, shocked me, and restored my heartbeat. GOD's mercy kept me.

On May 4, 2016, I was transferred and transported by a nurse and a police officer from Morgantown, West Virginia, to Butner, North Carolina. I maintained my integrity in JESUS CHRIST, that I will cut off occasion from those who desire occasion. I have been in pain, sickness, and weariness. For you will suffer if a man brings you into bondage and devour you, if a man takes advantage of you or exploits you. And I dare not make myself to be something that I am not or compare myself to some people who commend themselves. My suffering is good for the present time, but it cannot be compared with GOD's glory that is to be revealed.

## I Went to Prison for a Purpose

I went to prison for a purpose and for a reason. "To everything there is a season, and a time to every purpose under heaven." A time to be imprisoned, and a time to be released from prison. The LORD GOD has given travail to the sons of men to be exercised in it. For in the place of judgment, wickedness is right there. In the place where righteousness is said to be, there is iniquity. That which to be has already been done before, my GOD will call the past to account. GOD will bring into judgment, both the righteous and the wicked. I said to myself, as for us humans, the LORD GOD test us to let us be aware and see that we are just like animals.

> JESUS said, "Fear none of those things which you suffer; behold the Devil shall cast some of you in prison, that you may be tried; and you shall have tribulation ten days be thou faithful until death, and I will give you a crown of life." (Rev. 2:10)

> But my beloved, be not ignorant of this one thing that with the LORD one day is as a thousand years, and a thousand a thousand years is as a day. (2 Pet. 3:8)

> Therefore, since CHRIST suffered in the flesh [and died for us], arm your selves [like warriors] with the same purpose [being willing to suffer for doing what is right and pleasing [GOD] because whosoever has suffered in the flesh [being like-minded with CHRIST] is done with[intentional] sin [having stopped pleasing the world]. (1 Pet. 4:1)

While in prison, I found out that those who put me there had closed my business account, personal account, and the church account. They also sold the house. Simply put, I could not go back to College Park at this house where I had lived for thirteen and a half years. Having done three years in confinement, thoughts were going through my mind. They took the house; they took all my money; my wife divorced me; and I have one million in restitution, as they said. I kept asking the LORD, my Judge and Advocate, to show me how to get myself out of this dilemma I was in.

The LORD opened my understanding, and from Butner Prison Camp, I filed my 2016 taxes as directed. On Tuesday night, December 27, after the 9:00 p.m. count, I went to sleep. In the vision of the night, I dreamed that the state attorney was at the camp, outside the door. He was looking at some documents with one of my clients. Another man was standing behind him. Michael, with whom I became acquainted, was there with his attorney. Several prisoners were there, some sitting and some standing all around. I heard the state attorney with a loud voice say, "He won this one," speaking to my client. Then he said again, "I can't deny it! This is what rule E says. Why don't you men apply for release under rule E?"

I said to Michael and his attorney, "Should I ask him for my copy of the documents?"

We heard the state attorney say, "He will receive his copy. He is free. That's what the rule says."

I was speaking in tongues and giving glory to GOD. Everyone sitting and standing around looked at me in amazement as I praise the LORD in tongues.

Then I woke up from my sleep and wrote the dream down.

## A Very Present Help

I got on my knees and asked the LORD to send me help from His sanctuary to me with the Schedule F form. One Wednesday evening, in January of 2017, I was at the recreation center playing the guitar as I always do, giving praise to GOD. I was in the art room that has two doors, one with see-through glass, and two men were standing there looking at me.

One of them beckoned to me and asked, "May we come in?"

I nodded my head simultaneously with my lips saying yes.

They came in sat, and listened as I sang and praised the LORD.

I stopped the playing and said, "I am Julius Williams. I am here because GOD allowed it. I have been praying and asking the LORD to send me help. I also told them what my persecutors said that I did.

One of the men told me their names and said, "I was at the other side of the prison. While I was praying, the LORD told me, 'Someone over the Camp needs help.' That very morning, they called my name and told me to get ready to be taken over the Camp. We just came. I decided to come over here. I haven't unpacked my bag because somebody needs help. I will be leaving soon."

I said to him, "I prayed and asked GOD for help. I have some documents I started already. I can go and get them for you."

After I came back, he helped me complete the documents. Then I mailed them, one copy to the judge, one mailed to the Internal Revenue Service, and the other to the prosecutor.

After I had mailed the documents, I went to use the restroom. A voice echoed, saying, "Good news! The state attorney is a deacon."

I say to myself, "No, this can't be, not a deacon."

Again, the voice said to me, "The state attorney is a deacon."

I got out of the restroom and went to the library where the deacon was sitting with four other men.

I said, "Excuse me, deacon! I was in the restroom and the LORD spoke to me with a loud voice saying, 'The state attorney is a deacon."

He responded, "Yes, I am! The LORD told me to prosecute them, and that's what I'm doing."

This man was filled with the wisdom of GOD, and he has become a friend indeed. He got released in February, and I came out in May.

## The Release

After I got out from Butner, in North Carolina, I had to report to a halfway house in Augusta, Georgia. They kept me there tightly under wraps for thirty-seven days and sent me home, but they kept up their stunts and trickery with me. For a man who is not a drinker or a smoker, they had me doing drug test and peeing in cups. They came to my sister's place of residence to do their shenanigans.

They asked, "Do you have any weapons in the house?"

My sister said, "No."

I said, "Yes, I always have my weapon. By the way, there are lots of weapons in this house."

The officers panicked and said, "Where are the weapons?"

My sister, Dorseta, had three Bibles on the top of her piano. I reached for one and said, "Here is my weapon." Then I quoted 2 Corinthians 10:4, "For the weapon of my warfare are not the carnal weapons of the world; instead, they have divine power to demolish strongholds."

They were not talking about this weapon and were repugnant.

They tried everything in their power for me to doubt myself concerning the documents the LORD told me to file. After I left the halfway house, my final released date was September 21, 2018.

That Friday I went there for my release papers that I need to present to the probation officer. I went to the courthouse where the probation officer worked and met him. I presented to him the copy of the papers that I previously filed, sending one copy to the judge, one to IRS, and one to the prosecutor. When I handed him the paperwork for the payment, he asked me sarcastically, "What is this?"

I said, "This is my total payment for the restitution that the government said I owed them."

He pushed it aside and gave me a bunch of papers for financial and other personal information that I needed to produce. Then said he, "You need to pay the $100 partial payment." He left me sitting at the desk and came back with his manager.

He identified himself to me and asked me, "What is the problem?"

I took the envelope from the table with the paperwork and handed it to him.

He told the officer, "On Monday morning, take these papers to the IRS office and find out if they are any good."

The probation officer called me at home on Tuesday and said, "Mr. Williams, this is your probation officer. They said the papers that you filed aren't any good. You need to come see me and bring the $100 payment."

I said to him, "Sir, with all due respect, I will not be coming to see you. I already made the payment, and I gave you a copy. You can go ahead and do as you please. I am saying goodbye, and I will be hanging up the phone." I did not go back to see him. I kept in touch with the IRS to the best of my ability.

## My Meeting with the Revenue Officer

On March 19, 2019, I met with a revenue officer in Augusta, Georgia. She presented me with a bill for $1,391,819.47. I told her I already made the payment. And she said to me, "If you already filed the return, just wait until they process it." She gave me a copy of the document, and I left her office. When I came home, I signed the bill that I received from the revenue officer as I was directed and returned it to her.

One month later I received a letter from the officer. It stated,

> Case Closed—Currently Not Collectible. We determined you don't have the ability to pay the money you owed at this time. Although we have temporarily closed your case, you still owe the money to the IRS.

## The Wicked: My Enemies and My Foes

On April 23, 2019, I received this letter in the mail. It stated,

> Comes now S. H. PROBATION OFFICER OF THE COURT presenting an official report upon the conduct and attitude of Julius V. Williams who was placed on supervision for Aiding and Assisting in the Filing of False tax Returns, Wire

Fraud and aggravated Identity Theft, a Class E Felony, by the Honorable Paul W. Grimm, U.S. District Judge, sitting in the court at Greenbelt, Maryland, on the 11th day of February, 2015, who sentenced the defendant to 60 Months Bureau of Prisons; 36 Months Supervised Release, and imposed the general terms and conditions therefore adopted by the court and also imposed additional conditions and terms as follows:

Pursuant to 18 U.S.C.3583, the maximum penalty upon revocation is 1 year.

1.  The defendant shall provide the probation officer with access to any required financial information.
2.  The defendant shall not incur new credit charges or open additional lines of credit without the approval of the probation officer.
3.  The defendant shall cooperate with the Internal Revenue Service in determination of the civil tax liability and payment of any taxes, penalties, and interest that are due.
4.  Restitution: $1,000,000.00.
5.  The defendant shall not be employed as a tax preparer unless approved by the probation office.
6.  Special Assessment: $400.00.

## Presenting the Petition for Action of Court

RESPECTFULLY PRESENTING PETITION FOR ACTION OF COURT FOR (CAUSE AS FOLLOWS; violation # 1: On December 18, 2018, Mr. Williams failed to report to the probation officer as directed. The defendant is in violation of Standard Condition #2 which states: The defendant shall report to the probation officer in a manner and frequency directed by the court or probation officer.

Violation #2; To date, Mr. Williams has failed to make his monthly restitution payments of $100.00. He has an outstanding balance of $1,000,000.00.

The defendant is in violation of Statutory Condition #6 which states; If the judgment imposes any criminal monetary penalty, including special assessment, fine, or restitution, it shall in condition of supervised release that the defendant pay such monetary penalty that remains unpaid at the commencement of the term of supervised release in accordance with {the Schedule of Payment set forth in the Criminal Monetary Penalties sheet of this judgment. The defendant shall notify the court of any material change in the defendant's economic circumstances that might affect the defendant's ability to pay restitution, fines, or special assessments.

Violation #3; To date, Mr. Williams has failed to submit financial documents as directed by the probation office. The defendant is in violation of the Special Condition which states: The defendant shall provide the probation officer with access to any requested financial information.

Violation #4: In September 2018, Mr. Williams submitted false tax documents to the Internal Revenue Service.

The defendant is in violation of the Special Condition which states: The defendant shall cooperate with the Internal Revenue Service in the determination of the civil tax liability and the payment of any taxes, penalties, and interest that are due.

Praying that the court will order the issuance of a summons for the defendant to appear in court on May 2, 2019, at 11:00 am before the Honorable Thomas M. DiGirolamo, U.S. judge, for identification of counsel and setting of further revocation proceedings in order to show cause why Supervised Release should not be revoked.

## Order of Court

Considered and ordered this 15th day of April 2019, and ordered filed and made a part of the records in the above case.

On Thursday, April 25, 2019, I received the order signed by Judge Grimm to show up in court again. My sister, Dorseta, and I traveled from Augusta, Georgia, to Greenbelt, Maryland. We got to the courthouse and waited a few minutes. A man with white hair walked up to us and said to me, "Do you know who I am? You are a wise man. You are a good man. Why are you doing this by yourself? Those documents that you filed, they are no good."

I said to him, "I've never seen you before, and I don't know who you are."

He said, "I am the public defendant that came to help you."

I said to him, "The Lord is my helper. I filed the documents as I was told and made the payment."

The call was made. "The court is opened."

The public defender took us to an office before you enter in the courtroom and lectured me.

During his lecture, he pulled out some papers from his briefcase and gave me one copy and said, "Take this! Maybe it will help you."

I took the papers and put them in my coat pocket without reading them.

The court was now called to order, and we went in. After the acknowledgment of my presence in the court, the judge said to me,

"Mr. Williams, I want for you to know I am not here to accuse you or judge you. I have a document for you to sign acknowledging that you were here in the court. When you go back to Georgia, go and present yourself to the probation officer."

When we left the courthouse and I returned to the place where I stayed for the night, I took the document from my pocket and read it. Behold, it was the information in nature from which the state attorney used to finalize the filing of the documents for me while I was in Butner, North Carolina.

I laughed in amazement and said, "Is this a trick or what? How can you say to me, 'The documents that you filed are no good' and then you turned around and gave me the same document to help me. This just doesn't make any sense!"

The Lord revealed to me, "They are trying to trick you into forfeiting your rights."

## Satan, the Accuser of the Brethren

> And I heard a loud voice saying in heaven, "Now is come salvation, and strength, and the kingdom of our GOD, and the power of His Christ: for the accuser of our brethren is cast down, which accused them before our GOD day and night. And they overcame him by the blood of the Lamb, and by the word of their testimony; and they loved not their lives unto death. Therefore rejoice, ye heavens, and ye that dwell in them. Woe to the inhabiters of the earth and of the sea! For the Devil is come down unto you, having great wrath, because he knows that he has but a short time." (Rev. 12:10–12)

Propelled by the spirit of greed, lust, power, and control, they were determined to stop me at any cost. On September 4, 2019, some officer from Georgia Department of Revenue came by my sister's house and took me. They held me for three days, and then they let me go with the intent to pursue persecution

On October 29, 2019, I received this letter that stated:

> To remind you that the violation of supervised release hearing in your case remains set for Wednesday, November 6, 2019, at 2:30 p.m., before the Honorable Judge Paul W. Grimm, in Courtroom 4B of the U.S. District Court, located at 6500 Cherrywood Lane, Greenbelt, MD.

Knowing what the enemy is capable of doing you must be "strong in the LORD, and in the power of His might. Put on the whole armour of GOD, that you may be able to stand against the wiles of the devil" (Eph. 6:10–11).

When we got back to Georgia, I didn't go to see the probation officer. My reason for not going: the payment was already made. I presented myself before Judge Grimm on November 6, 2019.

When the court was called in session, the prosecutor got up and said, "Your Honor, the state of Georgia is requesting that you lock up Mr. Williams. He has violated his supervised release. Furthermore, Mr. Williams went back to Georgia and did not bother to go see the probation officer."

Judge Grimm said, "I will not make the same mistake as before. I will suggest to Mr. Williams that when he gets back to Georgia, he goes and see the probation officer."

The court was then adjourned.

You will notice that the court that gave the order for me to repay the one million dollars in monthly installments of $100.00 and this was to continue until 2023. So what would happen if I didn't payoff this money by 2023? I would still be held under their spell. Let's take a look at the double-standard behavior and hypocrisy of these people. The IRS says that I owed them $1,391,819.47. Both of them want me to pay what I had already paid. The devil is a scammer. He only comes to kill, steal, and destroy; but GOD grants deliverance.

My foes kept up their harassment, and I kept my faith in my GOD, JESUS CHRIST. On February 5, 2020, I received a letter from the public defender saying that I need to be present, not before Judge Grimm but before Judge Day. This was the judge that the prosecutor in the beginning had presented theories of lies in order to have me locked up. He was the one who said back then, "I-I hate to do this! I hate to do this! Marshals, he's in your hands."

Early in the morning of February 10, 2020, my sister, Dorseta, and I left Augusta, Georgia, and set out for Maryland.

On February 11, 2020, I went to face Judge Day. When the court was called into session, the public defender and I presented ourselves before the judge.

Judge Day said to me, "Mr. Williams, will you speak the truth?"

I replied, "I always speak the truth, sir."

The judge never ask me another question.

The prosecutor, Kelly Hayes, stood up and said, "Judge Day, Mr. Williams filed these documents with Judge Grimm's name all over them. He is still doing the same thing."

He interrupted her and said, "I don't want to talk about that. He doesn't listen to nobody." The judge was silent for a few minutes while he was writing something down. He then said to me, "Mr. Williams, remove your belt and your coat. Officer, come and take this man."

They always have two officers to take the prisoners. This time it was one officer who came for me; he was very gentle to me.

## They Tried to Break My Confidence

After they kept me downstairs of the courtroom for about ten minutes, they placed me in a van. Two hours later, the van pulled up at the DC jail in Southeast, Washington, DC.

When the officers got to the window to check me in, the two officers behind the shielded glass asked the officers, "Where is the paperwork that comes with the man?"

The two officers who accompanied me there said, "We have no documents nor paperwork. The judge told us to bring him here."

They checked me in under the old record in their computer system. Then the two officers brought me to the laundry department.

The officer sitting at the desk asked the officers, "Where is the paperwork?"

They replied, "We have no paperwork. The judge told us to bring him here."

The two officers then left the building.

Another officer came to check me in for my clothing and to give me my bedding and hygiene. He again asked for a copy of the paperwork that should have accompanied me. He said to me, "What is your name, sir?"

"My name is Julius Williams," I said.

He said, "Mr. Williams, what did you do? Did you piss off the judge?"

I briefly told him a part of my story, how the LORD JESUS CHRIST vindicated me and showed me how to pay the restitution, which I did, but they were trying to break my confidence.

He said to me, "You will not be here for long. You are a good man. You are a man of faith, and you fear GOD. You will be out very soon." He then told the other officer who came to replace him for that shift, "This is Mr. Williams. He is a good man. Please to take good care of him."

They kept me at that section of the prison for two weeks. Then on February 27, 2020, they moved me to the next building, in a section called Medical 96.

As soon as they brought me there, even though I felt jaded and my heart was burdened, I started to sing, "JESUS dropped the charges." The prisoners heard, and some joined with me. Not too long after being there, the coronavirus pandemic began, and all activities were cancelled.

This is the report that was in the news:

As of Sunday, May 3, 2020, 152 prisoners tested positive with coronavirus. One prisoner died; one jail employee died. As of Sunday, 61 Department of Corrections employees had been infected. As of Sunday, 86 employees are off work, testing positive or quarantined after having come in contact with someone infected.

It was this place, in the TV room, that the LORD showed me on the wall, "The coronavirus pandemic was created to hurt President Donald Trump in the upcoming election."

Several prisoners were released because of the virus. The public defender sent me a letter, saying, "I asked the court for an Emergency Motion under the COVID-19 pandemic."

This was the court's response to the public defender:

> The Court is not persuaded that Defendant has demonstrated by clear and convincing evidence that he should be released from detention. The combination of his age and the existence of COVID-19, standing alone, are not sufficient for the reasons stated above. Accordingly, Defendant's Emergency Motion is *denied*. So ordered this 23rd day of March, 2020.

The attorney wrote to me, saying, "Dear Mr. Williams, I write to inform you that the emergency motion for consideration of bond was denied by the court on April 16th. A copy of the memorandum order is enclosed. I am saddened by this decision. Please know that despite this setback, I'll continue to fight for you and all clients."

I asked one of the officers for the privilege to call the public defender. The privilege was granted. I called the number, and a young lady answered.

"Is this Mr. Williams? How are you? Are they treating you any good?

I said, "Not really, but my GOD is treating me really, really good."

She said, "Hold for Mr. Chamble."

He answered the phone, saying. "Mr. Williams, how may I help you today? Did you receive my letter?"

I said to him, "Yes, sir. But I didn't ask you to do that. I need for you to put in a dismissal for me."

He said to me, "You know the judge is not a fan of yours, right? Nevertheless, at your word, I will."

I said to him, "Thank you, sir," and I hanged up the phone.

## It Is Over because God Said It's Over

The request was made to the court, and a virtual hearing was scheduled for July 8, 2020. At this hearing were the probation officer, court reporter, prosecutor, public defender, and the judge. I was given three minutes to consult with the attorney, who said to me, "Mr. Williams, smile! It's going to be over today. The judge told me this morning that he had an encounter with you. When you go before him, you only have three questions to answer. Just answer yes, and let's get this thing over with."

I said, "Yes, sir."

"We are going into court," Attorney Chamble said.

Then the judge said, "Mr. Williams, can you hear me?"

"Yes, Your Honor," I said.

Judge Grimm then said, "It is said, that Defendant failed to report to the probation officer in a manner and frequency directed by the court or probation officer, how do you plea?"

Then said I, "Guilty, Your Honor."

"It is said, Defendant failed to make his monthly restitution payments of $100 statutory condition 6. How do you plea?"

Then said I, "Guilty, Your Honor."

"It is said, Defendant failed to provide the probation officer with access to any requested financial information. How do you plea?"

I responded, "Guilty, Your Honor."

Then said Judge Grimm, "Supervised release is revoked. The Defendant is discharged as to such violation no. 4 of petition 1 dated April 19, 2019; violation no. 5 of petition 2 dated November 7, 2019; and violation no. 6 of petition 3 dated February 6, 2020.

One million dollars is revoked." The judge then asked all the parties involved, "Are you all in agreement with the decision?"

They all said, "Yes, we are in agreement, Your Honor."

The judge said to me, "Mr. Williams, sometime ago you and I had an encounter. I hope you have a good life, and I hope I never see you again in my life." Then the judge continued, "Anyone has anything else to say?"

I said, "Me, Your Honor! I need my passport, please."

He replied, "The attorney will take care of it for you. This court is adjourned."

# THIS IS
# AWESOME

## Allow God to Bring Justice into Your Life

The LORD has a promise made: if we will put our trust and confidence in Him, He will pay us back for all the unjust things that we have happened to us. You might have been cheated on in a business deal and a lot of money has been lost. Someone might have lied on you, and that twisted information kept you back from your promotion. You might have had friends that turned their backs and betrayed you. Or maybe friends or family betrayed and robbed you to your face.

All these kind of losses leave you with irrevocable scars, pressuring you to hold on to your pain and your grief. And the first thought that comes to your mind is revenge. Your friends may encourage you to take out your revenge on them. Now you have even the score, and you do see a lot of this happening today. Surely the LORD has a plan. So if you believe the best is yet to come, you have to allow the LORD time for your justice. "Vengeance is mine; I will repay," says the LORD.

How far you have come, never forget. Do not forget everything you have gotten through. When folks have hurt you to the core, "bless them which persecute you, and say all manner of evil things against you, bless them and curse not." The LORD will always settle every case for His people. You don't have to take matters into your own hands, paying people back for their wrongs. The LORD is your Judge. Do you believe it? He is true and honest. He is the only righteous Judge. None other is righteous—no, not one. They are all gone out of the right way. The LORD has no respect for any one's person.

Will you be patient and allow the LORD to take control and settle your battles and your cases on time and in time? He will surely bring justice into your life and make your wrongs right. When you are at your wits end, you feel you have reached a road block, and you feel like turning around, please don't give up! Push on just the same.

The road block will be cleared soon. Turning back will never allow you to reach your intended destination. You have feelings of doom, but if you keep your mind on your destination, good things and thoughts will come into focus. And very, very soon you have reached your destination, and now you are glad you never turned around.

For every temptation and test is an occasion to trust GOD. If you want GOD to lead, you must be willing to follow. No danger can come so near that GOD is not nearer. For every one of us, the LORD has a plan for you, to do you good and not evil. Just remember giving up and turning around is not a good idea and will only have a negative effect on your peers, friends, and others. But as you push ahead, getting over the road blocks, you find yourself reaching out to others and helping them reach out to GOD. Just as the Word of GOD has power to save, your word has power to influence.

## The Lord Will Bring Justice into Your Life

It takes a lot of courage and just a little faith to believe that the LORD really wants to vindicate you. Do not allow yourself to be brought down to your offenders and persecutors' level, arguing and fighting, which will only make matters worse. Let the LORD take control. In the end, you will be better off than you were before. Strengthen yourself in the LORD. Only then you will be able to say to those who are of a fearful heart, be strong, fear not. Your GOD will come with vengeance, even JESUS CHRIST with a recompence. He will bring justice into your life. You will find yourself opening the spiritual eyes of the blind, and the ears of the deaf will be unstoppable.

"For evildoer will be cut off but those that wait upon the LORD, has an inheritance." Just take a little time out and be patient. The wicked that you see today, it won't be long. The LORD will render His justice on your behalf. The LORD knows that their day is coming. He wants us to do justice and judgment. Do you not believe he will render justice for you? If He did it before, He will do it again. GOD's justice will run down like a stream. All those that have formed a confederacy in consent behind your back, you don't have to worry. The LORD will bring justice into your life. As the fire burns wood and as the flames set mountains on fire, so will the LORD persecute them and bring justice into your life. The LORD will allow those who troubled you to be confounded. With tempest will He persecute them and make them to be afraid of His storm. He just blows on them and brings justice into your life.

"For yet a little while and the wicked shall not be." The LORD will give to them that which is good. The LORD brings justice by elevating and lifting up people. The LORD is a good recordkeeper.

## The LORD is a good recordkeeper

When the LORD wants for you to be elevated in promotion, it makes no difference who it is that is trying to bring injustice into your life. Your life is not contingent on what people do or doesn't do. Just remember that your justice and your promotion does not come from the north, south, east, or the west. Whether there is a company or no company at all, your justice and promotion will come. The LORD is not unjust.

Many times, the LORD test you going through the situation. Right now, you may have something in your life or someone who is not treating you right. It might very well be your faith is put to the test. Will you be angry, bitter, become negative, or develop a vindictive attitude, always fighting back? Or are you going to turn it over to the LORD, trusting Him to make your wrong right? Will you pass your test so that the LORD will bring justice into your life and promote you? Maybe your coworkers or your boss and all your left-wing associates and friends are not treating you right. You are doing your very best and not getting any credit at all. Everyone is receiving justice, moving up except you. You may be tempted to pout and have a sour attitude. You need to trust the LORD to make up for you instead. You are not just on the job to please your coworkers. Your trial, test, and your troubles will always affect someone else.

Whatever you do, do it as unto the LORD, not unto men and women. You are not merely working for your boss or for that company. You are really working for the LORD. He sees every wrong that's being done to you. The LORD is a good recordkeeper. He is watching your behavior. He is closely monitoring your situation, and He said that he will repay. The LORD repays in abundance, and there is nothing anyone can do about it.

When the LORD is promoting and repaying you because your time is fully come to advance up the ladder, the powers of darkness and spiritual wickedness in high places cannot hold you down or prevent you. The LORD GOD requires of us to do justice, and justice you will receive. It does not mean if after a week, or month, or a year, or even more, you don't see anything happening, you can become manipulative, taking matters into your own hands. When we do, we always interrupt GOD's plan and purpose. Now we leave a mess for the LORD to clean up or prevent us from getting our breakthrough because of our attitude.

"GOD Almighty knows I pray, pay my tithes, working myself, doing two person's job. And it seems I am not progressing," Charmaine quipped. "Things are looking good for everyone around me. When is it going to be my turn, brother Williams?"

Whatever your hands find to do, just do it with all your might and murmur not. "I know the thoughts that I think toward you," says the LORD. "Thoughts of peace, and not of evil, to give you an expected end. Then shall you call upon Me, and shall go and pray unto Me, and I will hearken unto you."

Don't stop praying, for the LORD is near. What He has promised, that will He do. Many times, you feel tired, worn-out. I will just stay in bed. You then find the strength to get out no matter how hard it is. The LORD GOD gave you strength for the day and made a way for you when you saw no way.

## GOD knows what He is thinking toward you

Just one touch of GOD's favor and things turn around; and you are put in charge of a company or organization, making up for all the hard work you have done. It doesn't matter how people are treating you, holding you back, ignoring you, and holding you down. Just keep doing the right thing. Don't be offended. Don't let anyone get you upset. Don't return evil for evil.

The LORD GOD knows they have said some horrible things about you. They have slaughtered you with their tongue. They are murderers, and the LORD will unleash His vengeance upon them very soon. You just do the right thing. Speak kindly and respond to everyone in love. And because of your actions, when the time comes for promotions, the LORD will make it happen. Everything that you deserve, the LORD will give you! "No good thing will He withhold from them that walk uprightly." This is awesome!

## Just turn it over to GOD

Some bad and nasty things have been said behind your back, some of them you heard. "No big deal" should be your attitude. The LORD will make it up for me. He got me covered. Don't be downcast or perplex if someone cheats you and robbed you out of your money or other property. Let them have it. The LORD will restore you with twice as much, or more.

All the bad and wrong that happened to you, don't try to fix them. Let JESUS fix it for you. He knows just what to do. Get out of the way, and let JESUS fix it for you. When you have confidence that the LORD is in control, you'll get out of the way and let Him do the driving. He will fight your battles and make all your wrongs right. You must understand that we serve a GOD who can and will do more than you can ask or think. Forget about how people are treating you. Just don't forget about GOD. He didn't forget about you. He is always looking out for you, always busy opening doors that you just can't see. You don't have to worry, for He's taking care of your business for you.

If you will leave your situation up to the LORD, in the end, you will come out better than you were before. You will be amazed how far ahead you have reached. Truly, the LORD can bring changes and justice into your life. So don't you worry. Don't you fret about those whom have robbed you and are prospering in their robbery. They shall soon be cut down like the grass and wither as green herbs. Not for one moment do you ever have to worry about that person. Fret not yourself because of that person who is prospering in his way because of his or her wicked devices. Delight yourself in the LORD. Without a doubt, He will give you the desires of your heart. Keep on looking up to GOD. Oh, how much He cares for you. If you have the Spirit of GOD dwelling in you, you are a potent commodity to the LORD. You are not just a mere ordinary person; you are spectacular, and you are royal. You have been bought with the precious blood of JESUS CHRIST, the lamb of GOD who takes away the sins of the world.

## Don't Blame God, Only Trust Him

While I was in Morgantown, West Virginia, I met a young man in the prison camp who was always singing about GOD. Each time he heard me sing, he would join in or give me a compliment. Whenever I spoke the Word of God, he would say, "Man, GOD is awesome. I don't know what I would do without Him." After about six months worshipping together, he went missing. One month had passed, and he returned to the camp in a wheelchair with a bag and a tube inserted into his abdomen. This bag was to carry his feces because of some abnormal condition in his body.

One Saturday evening, I went to brush my teeth, and this young man was in the chair waiting for his pusher. Not seeing him for a while, I said, "Hello, my friend, how are you doing?"

He didn't respond to me.

Again, I said to him, "How are you doing?"

He paid me no mind at all.

His neighbor came in and said, "Hello, buddy, it's good to see you. GOD is good, man. You are back and alive."

He responded to his neighbor and said, "Don't talk to me about GOD. I don't want to hear about Him. If GOD was so good, why did He allow me to come to prison? And look at me now. I can't go to bathroom as I would like. I can't even walk. Someone have to be pushing me. So don't you stand there telling me that GOD is good. Keep Him to yourself and leave me alone."

The enemy did a number on this young man. He was mad and upset with GOD. Now every time I see him or go by him, he would be cursing and swearing and wishing he were dead.

After a few times greeting him without any response, I left him alone.

Eight months passed, and there was no communication between us. On my way to the restroom someone said to me, "Brother Williams, could I speak with you for a moment?"

I turned around and saw this young man pushing himself in the wheelchair.

I said, "How are you? What can I do for you?"

He said, "Can you pray for me, please? I don't know what I've been thinking. I am so depressed."

So I prayed for him and reassured him that the LORD loves him and had forgiven him of his sins. I invited him to worship with the brothers the next Sunday evening. He came, and we laid hands on him and anointed him with oil in the name of JESUS CHRIST. The Great GOD turned his situation around. There is no limit what GOD can do. Don't blame GOD, only trust Him. He will save you now.

If you are totally honest with yourself, you will find out that your problem is really you. And if you never had a problem, you'd never know that GOD could solve them. You may be experiencing some very difficult times. Perhaps your circumstances and the situation have seem stagnant for quite a while. You are not able to understand how your condition or the situation can ever move forward. Be this known unto you: the LORD has the answer to all that you are going through, even before you had that need. Before you ever encountered that need, the LORD has been arranging things in your favor.

If you steal and get caught, don't blame GOD. If you burglarized a home or a business and get caught, don't you blame GOD. If you commit fraud and get caught, don't blame GOD. If you have been dealing in drugs or is associated with someone who is involved in it and you get caught, don't blame GOD. If you have been caught with an illegal weapon, don't blame GOD. If you used your illegal weapons to commit your crimes and you end up behind bars, don't you for one moment blame GOD. When you stepped in front of a mirror and you take a look in it, tell me what do you see? You see yourself looking back at you. This is truly awesome!

# Find Me a Culprit

No one wants to take responsibility for their actions. And in this world that we are living in today, the odium is widespread. I will do whatever it takes to get what I desire, and the rest, I blame it on you. He that knoweth how to do good and doeth it not will be beaten with many stripes. You don't have to worry about blaming anyone when you are doing right. The sad truth is, if you keep on pushing hard enough in the wrong direction and if you're so stubborn that you must have things your way, GOD will allow you to go along with your bad self and undertake your project, and you end up suffering the consequences. When your heart is evil, the whole man is evil. So what should I be expecting from you? What if my expectation is not met?

The problem with that is, when you start something in your own strength and your own timing, you will do badly, finishing it in your own strength. My GOD will always give you the desires of your heart.

> See, I have set before you this day life and good, and death and evil. I call heaven and earth to record this day against you, that I have set before you life and death, blessing and cursing; therefore choose life, that both you and your seed may live. (Deut. 30:15, 19)

If you have made poor choices that lands you into the doldrums of the prison system, and you happen to get out, just ask the Savior to help, comfort, strengthen, and save you. I am sure He'll see you through. GOD has set before you length of days. Why should you die before your time? If your suffering is for doing your evil acts and deeds, you must bear and suffer the consequences. It will be nobody's fault but yours. If your prison time was for that which was right, what do you have to worry about? You should be happy, and don't worry yourself about all the terror the officers, prisoners, and the system brings. Glorify GOD and lift Him up in praise.

If you are in an area or situation like this today, you need to ask the LORD to help you do your best to get out of there. For that is not a place of contentment and satisfaction. Every man's work shall be clearly seen in that day or the day you are caught. You need to amend your ways and your doings. Obey the voice of GOD. I guarantee you, my GOD will repent of what He has caused the enemy to put you through. If you are put to death and it is a consequence of your bad, detestable, and your violent behavior, you have received the fruit of your doing. But know for sure, that if they put you to death and you are innocent, they will surely bring your innocent blood upon themselves.

## My God Is Awesome

My GOD is awesome! He is great in counsel and mighty in His works. His eyes are upon all the ways of the sons and daughters of men, and everyone will receive according to the fruit of deeds, actions, according to your ways. When you are doing that which is right or striving to do right, He will be with you as a mighty terrible one to take out His revenge on those causing chaos in your life. Your persecutors shall stumble, and they shall not prevail against you. They shall be ashamed. They shall not prosper.

As the prosecutor brings you before the judge to try you and, if found guilty, to punish you; so the LORD test and examine the righteous and probe the heart and mind. He rescues the needy from the hands of the wicked. If you are very, very wicked, there is hope for you. Isaiah 55:7 says, "Let the wicked forsake his way, and the unrighteous man his thoughts and let him return to the LORD, and He will have mercy upon you, our GOD will abundantly pardon you." GOD is looking at your ways and wants to heal you and restore you. Will you allow Him to do that for you?

You have wearied yourself in the greatness of your foolish way and you are now at a place where nobody cares, will you just die or ask the Savior to help you? I am not pessimistic; I am an optimist. Just take a look at me. The awesome GOD has set me free. He washed all my sins away. He has opened up my blinded eyes and set me to rejoice, and I am so confident He will do the very same for you. Just let go and let GOD have His way in your life. When you receive good advice and the counsel of the wise and will not take heed, you will be laughed at in your calamity.

*The wicked will continue in their wickedness,*
*but the awesome GOD will deliver*

Many years ago, there was a convention of the Apostolic Church of JESUS CHRIST, in uptown Kingston, Jamaica. There were many delegates in attendance. The convention started on Sunday and ended Friday. After the closure of worship on Thursday night, a young sister, alone, was on her way home. When she reached the National Heroes Park Cemetery, the overhead streetlight was out of service. Out of the dark, a young man approached her and stuck a gun in her neck, held her by the hand and said, "Don't you ever scream." The gate to the cemetery at that location was broken. The young man said to the sister, "Go straight ahead in the park. I am going to rape you tonight." She went along while he had the gun pointed at her. When they got in the park, he said, "Take your clothes off now." She did not! So he pushed the gun in her neck again and said, "I told you to strip." With the gun stuck in neck, she closed her eyes and lift up her hands to heaven and said, "JESUS, JESUS!" He pushed the gun up some more in her neck and said, "Don't you ever call that name again. I said, strip!" Again, with her eyes closed, she cried out, saying, "JESUS, JESUS, JESUS." Then she opened her eyes. The young man was gone, and she was standing there by herself. She just walk out the park and went merrily on her way home.

## Be Not Afraid, Only Believe, God Is Awesome

The next night, Friday, she went back for the final night of worship. After the singing and the testimonies, the preacher preached the word. In the end, the pastor called for all those who wanted to make a change, by giving their lives to the LORD JESUS. A young man walked up and asked the pastor if he could say something. The pastor handed him the mike.

The young man said, "I have a confession to make. Last night a sister from this church was on her way home. I went up to her and held her by the hand and took her to the cemetery park in the dark. I told her to strip. She did not. So I pushed the gun in her neck and said, 'I say strip.' She cried out and called on JESUS three times. When I looked around, soldiers were all around us with guns pointing at me. I saw an open spot where there was no one. I ran before they could shoot me."

The pastor said, "And what would you like the LORD to do for you tonight?"

"I want the LORD to save me. I want to be baptized in the name of JESUS CHRIST. I want to be saved."

The pastor called one of the deacons, "Take this man and baptize him. He wants to be saved."

The deacon took the man baptized him in the name of JESUS CHRIST. While he was coming up out of the water, he was speaking in tongues and praising GOD.

After this, the young man submitted himself to the LORD. Some time had passed, and he ended up marrying the sister and have been enjoying life. There is no need for him to use a gun. Now he has her all to himself. GOD protected her from him and saved him for her, for he stated, "Soldiers were all around us with guns pointing at me. I saw an open spot where there was no one. I ran before they could shoot me." Only GOD can take your mess and turn it into a message that is for edification. Only GOD can turn your test into a testimony. Only GOD can turn your trial into your triumph. And GOD will take you as a victim and make you a victor. GOD loves you without limitation. This is truly awesome.

We are so convinced we know what is best for us. We are so convinced we know all the things we need. But you know nothing until you know GOD's love that he brought down to fallen man and lifted you up from out of the sin where you have fallen. GOD want for you to know just how it feels to trust and depend on Him. He knows your need before you even ask Him. As I have previously stated, I will say it again, all that we need the LORD has provided. He has given us choices.

He will never force you to come to Him to be saved. You need to feel the urge. For everything in your life there is an urge. Those who know the name of the LORD must be hungry for Him. "My soul thirsts for GOD, for the living GOD (Ps. 142:2).

# WILL YOU MAKE THE AWESOME GOD YOUR REFUGE?

## Your Refuge Is God

If you say, "The LORD is my refuge," and you make the awesome GOD your dwelling, no harm will overtake you. No disaster will come near your home. The awesome GOD will command His angels concerning you to guard you in all your ways. Because you set your attention and your love upon GOD, He will deliver you. GOD will set you up because you know His name. There is nothing He can't solve for you. When you have tried your best and the rest comes in on you and try you, how will you fare? You don't have to go out to be tested. The test will come your way.

When you look all around you, confusion is everywhere. Men and women have made this world into a terrible place. You don't have to worry if you make the awesome GOD your refuge. He reigns from heaven above with His love, His power, and His wisdom. If you are rebellious, don't exalt yourself. The LORD is terrible in His doings toward you and me.

> For Thou, O GOD, has proved us: Thou has tried us as silver is tried. Thou brought us into the net; Thou laid affliction upon our loins. Thou has caused men to ride over our heads; we went through fire and through water; But Thou brought us out into a wealthy place. I hope that you have not too quickly forgotten that the LORD GOD is your refuge and your strength.

## He Will Save You, He Is Awesome

In 1989, Hamis came from Jamaica to spend some time with my wife and me. She was willing to have me share the Word of GOD

139

with her. As we sat at the dining table and communed, she said, "Brother Williams, how can you say that JESUS is GOD when He Himself said He is the Son of GOD? And how can you say one can only be saved only if they are baptized in the name of JESUS CHRIST, when JESUS said, 'Go ye therefore, and teach all nations, baptizing them in the name of the Father, and of the Son, and of the Holy Ghost.' Are you saying that my mother who is sixty-five years old and has been an Adventist all her life is not saved?"

I said to her, "Who am I talking with? You or your mother?"

She said, "You are talking to me."

I said, "Good. What if I can show you in the Word that JESUS is GOD and that all the baptisms in the book of the Acts of the Apostles (actions of the apostles) were done in the name of JESUS CHRIST, will you allow Him to be your Savior and refuge?"

She said to me, "Brother Williams, if you can show me that JESUS is GOD and that the baptism is in the name of JESUS CHRIST and not Father, Son, and Holy Ghost, I will let you baptize me."

My wife was in the kitchen preparing dinner. I called her to join us in prayer. We prayed and went into the Word. As we journeyed through the Word, she said to me, "Oh my! JESUS is truly GOD. So why people keep on lying, saying that He is not GOD? Are they lying, or they just don't know? I want for you to baptize me tomorrow."

Sunday morning came, and we went to worship at the Mount Olivet Apostolic Church in Washington, D.C. She was immersed in water in the name of JESUS CHRIST by Elder Anthony Morris.

Sunday evening while we were in the apartment, sister Hamis went to pray. Soon after, she started calling, "JESUS, JESUS, JESUS, JESUS." Then she started speaking with tongues as the Spirit gave her utterance. The Spirit of the LORD was moving in the building. He moved on my wife and me, and we started speaking with tongues just as sister Hamis was doing. I called four mothers of the church that I know to be filled with the Spirit of GOD. They all started speaking with tongues when they heard the sister speaking, "Our GOD is an awesome GOD." Sister Hamis stayed with us for two weeks and went back to Jamaica.

A month later, she called to give us her report.

"I went to worship at my mother's church. After I went in, the pastor said to me, 'Sister Hamis, I see that you are back. Do have a word of testimony for us?' I got up, greeted the church, and said, 'I thank GOD for filling me with the power of the Holy Ghost with the evidence of speaking with other tongues in the US. Thank GOD for saving me.' And then I spoke in tongues as the Spirit moved in me. The pastor said to me, 'My sister, sit down! You are mad. You can't stay in this church. You have to leave.' I did as he said. I went and found a spirit-filled church where I am worshipping now.'" Then she said, "Do you want to hear something else?"

I said, "Oh yes, I do."

She said, "I went to look for my sister uptown. On my way back, I took a bus heading downtown. Then the bus stopped. A young man with dreadlocks walked in and sat beside me. He had a bottle in his hand. He pulled up close to me, and I felt a hard object pressing on me, but I ignored him. He said to me, 'I need the ring on your finger. I have acid in this bottle, and I have a gun with me.' I said, 'What did you say bwoy? You must be out of your mind.' He opened the bottle, and I cried, 'JESUS.' I started speaking in tongues as the Spirit of GOD moved in me. I heard the bwoy said, 'Driver, please to stop the bus. You have a mad woman inside here.' The driver stopped the bus, and the man got off. My GOD is so good to me. Thank GOD for the Holy Ghost."

## Watch This!

Simon Peter and John both went to worship at the temple called Beautiful. A young man that came out of his mother's womb lame was placed at the gate. Peter and John observed this man and discerned that he had enough faith to receive his blessing. They gave him a command, "Look on us." He was obedient and looked. They commanded him to rise up in the name of JESUS CHRIST and walk. He received strength in his ankle bone and his feet, and he leaped up and walked. Some of the people were amazed and filled with excitement. Others were amazed and not happy.

They were looking at Peter and John in amazement as though it was their own power, but they set the record straight.

"What you just saw happened to this young man is faith. Through the name and in the name of Jesus Christ has made the young man strong and sound in your presence."

Some folks love truth, and most people hate the truth. You are bold, have faith in your God. You are not afraid to let the world of people know that you believe in telling and standing for the truth:

> For Moses truly said unto the people, "A Prophet shall the Lord your God raise up unto you of your brethren, like unto me; Him shall you hear in all things whatsoever he shall say unto you.' And it shall come to pass, that every soul(person), which will not hear that Prophet, shall be destroyed from among the people. To you God raised His Son (God Himself) Jesus, send Him to bless you, in turning you away from every one of your iniquities." (Acts 3:22–25)

## Peter and John versus human resistance

The powers that be in Peter and John's time should be glad healing was taking place and the Word of God was been taught. But they were grieved that they were teaching the people that Christ rose from the dead. They arrested them and brought them before the judgment seat. They were demanded to make known who gave them power to do their work. Then Peter, filled with the Holy Ghost, said unto them, "You rulers of the people and elders of Israel, if we this day be examined of the good deed done to the impotent man, by what means he is made whole. Be it known unto you all the people of Israel, that by the name of Jesus Christ of Nazareth, whom you crucified, whom God raised from the dead, even by Him does this man stand here before you whole. This is the stone which was set at nought by you builders, He is become the head of the corner. There is neither salvation in any other name under heaven given among men, whereby we must be saved." When they saw the boldness of Peter and John and perceived that they were unlearned and ignorant men, they marveled. They took knowledge of them that they have been with JESUS.

And looking at the man that was healed standing with them, they could say nothing against it. So they ordered them to withdraw from the Sanhedrin and then conferred together.

"What shall we do to these men?" they asked. "Everyone living in Jerusalem knows they have performed a notable miracle, and we cannot deny it. But to stop this from spreading any further among the people, we must threaten them to speak no longer to anyone in this name."

Then they called them in again and commanded them not to speak nor teach at all in JESUS's name.

But Peter and John replied, "Which is right in GOD's eyes, to listen to you or Him? You be the judges! As for us, we cannot help speaking about what we have seen and heard."

After further threats, they let them go. They could not decide how to punish them because all the people were praising GOD for what had happened. For the man that was miraculously healed was over forty years old. On their release, Peter and John went back to their own people and reported all that the chief priest and elders had said unto them. When they heard this, they raised their voices together in prayer to GOD. After they prayed, the place where they were meeting was shaken. And they were all filled with the Holy Ghost and spoke the Word of GOD boldly (Acts 4). And more believers were added to the LORD, men and women. They healed a lot of sick folks. Crowds gathered from the towns around Jerusalem, bringing their sick, and those tormented by unclean spirits were healed.

## The apostles are arrested

The high priest and all their associates who were members of the party of the Sadducees were filled with jealousy. They arrested the apostles and put them in the public jail. During the night, an angel of the LORD opened the doors of the jail and brought them out. "Go, stand in the temple courts and tell the people all about this life."

At daybreak, they entered the temple, as they were told, and began to teach the people. The high priest and his associates arrived. They called together the Sanhedrin, the full assembly of the elders of Israel, and sent the two apostles to the jail. But on their arrival at the jail, the officers did not find them.

They returned and told them, "We found the doors securely locked, with the guards standing there, but when we opened the doors, we found no one inside."

On hearing this, they were worried, wondering what this might lead to. Then someone came and said, "Look! The men you put in jail are standing in the temple courts teaching the people."

The captain went with the officers and brought the apostles without force or violence before the council.

The high priest said to them, "We gave you strict orders not to teach in this name. Yet you have filled Jerusalem with your teaching and are determined to make us guilty of this man's blood."

Then Peter and the other apostles answered, "We ought to obey GOD rather than human beings. The GOD of our ancestors raised JESUS from the dead, whom you killed by hanging Him on a cross. GOD exalted Him to His own right hand as Prince and Savior that He might bring Israel to repentance and forgive their sins. We are witnesses of these things, and so is the Holy Ghost, whom GOD has given to those who obey Him."

When they heard this, they were furious and wanted to put them to death. But a Pharisee named Gamaliel, a teacher of the law, who was honored by all the people, stood up in the council and ordered that the men be put outside for a little while. He said unto them, "You men of Israel, take heed to your selves what you intend to do to these men. Some time ago Theudas boasting himself to be somebody, and about four hundred men joined him. He was killed! All his followers were scattered and came to nothing. After him, Judas came in the days of the census and led a band of people in revolt. He too was killed, and his followers were scattered. Now, in this present case, I advise you leave these men alone! Let them go! For if their purpose and work is of human power, it will fail. If it is of GOD, you will find yourselves fighting against Him, and you will not be able to stop these men."

They were persuaded by his speech. Nonetheless, they called the apostles in, whipped them, commanded them not to speak in the name of JESUS, and let them go. The apostles went out from their presence with joy, rejoicing that they had suffered shame for the name of JESUS. Day after day, they went into the temple courts and from house to house. They never stopped teaching and preaching that JESUS CHRIST is GOD.

It is hard for you to fight against GOD. You will come to naught. With JESUS, there is too much to gain to lose. Keep holding on.

For you never know what lies around the bend. You are up today, and tomorrow your life may end. Whatever you do and wherever you go, don't take this life for granted. You never know when your life will end.

## With Jesus There Is Too Much to Gain to Lose

You are going through your heartaches, your pains, and your struggles. Your belief and faith in JESUS will not be in vain. Having this assurance that the best is yet to come, JESUS will come and will not tarry. For you shall receive power, and after that, the Holy Ghost will come upon you. Living without the Holy Ghost is lifeless. Living with the Holy Ghost is Christ in you, the hope of glory. You have this hope as an anchor for the soul, firm and secure. It enters the inner sanctuary (the heart) behind the curtain (body), where our forerunner, JESUS, entered on our behalf.

Your deliverance will come. Your physical body life will come to an end. A man who dies will surely live again but not by your own doings. There is going to be a time of trouble, but trouble won't last always. Everyone who believes in JESUS and do His will, will be delivered, if your name is written in the book of life. At this moment, many are asleep in the dust of the earth, just waiting for the best to come. Some, the righteous, shall awake to gain everlasting life. The others will remain in the earth to receive a reward of shame and everlasting contempt.

## The call for your election is now

The story told of two friends who met and talked for a while, then they went their separate ways. They had hoped to meet again someday if the good LORD will have it that way. So one day he called her phone to say a nice hello. She had died, and he did not know. He inquired and got the bad news that his friend had died. He got dressed and went to pay his respect and see her last remain. On reaching the house of worship, his life came to an end. He never know that his life would so soon end.

To make your election sure, you need to "seek the LORD while He may be found." "Repent and be baptized, everyone in the name JESUS CHRIST, and you shall receive the gift of the Holy Ghost," and your election may be sure. You must continue to do the right thing until you die. They that continue to the end shall be saved. "Be ye therefore steadfast, unmoveable, always abounding in the work of the LORD, for as much as you know that your labor is not in vain in the LORD."

Because of Adam's disobedience (sin), all died. But he that believes and is trusting in JESUS until he dies, shall live. "As it is written: For JESUS sake we are killed all day long; we are considered as sheep to be slaughtered" (Rom. 8:36) "Be sober, be vigilant, because your adversary the devil, as a roaring lion, walking about, seeking whom he may devour." I will live and not die.

## Look at the mystery

We were given a body like Adam, and he lived for 930 years and died. We too have an appointment with death. JESUS body had no corruption and could not die. As we bore the image of the earthly, we shall also bear the image of the heavenly (JESUS). Wherein we have already sinned, let us awake to righteousness. The best that is yet to come cannot be inherited with blood and flesh. Only the miserable, senseless, and unbelievers have their hope in this life. A change is about to take place.

Your corruptible body must put on incorruption. Your mortal body must put on immortality. Death and the grave will not have the victory over you. The LORD JESUS CHRIST has given us the victory. "For what is our hope, or joy, or crown of our rejoicing?" I cry with those that cried. I mourn with those that mourned. I have sorrows as those who have sorrows. I weep with those that weep.

The LORD make us to increase and abound in love toward all men—to the end. That He may establish your heart without blame in holiness before GOD, even the Father. The best is yet to come. So when the enemy comes with death, because you choose life, you do not weep for the dead as those who have no hope.

First Thessalonians 4:14–18, says,

> If you believe that JESUS died and rose again, even so them also which sleep in JESUS will GOD bring with Him. According to the Word of the LORD, we which are alive and remain alive spiritually will not prevent those who are asleep. For the LORD Himself will come down from heaven with a loud command, with the voice of the arc angel and with the trumpet of GOD, and the dead in CHRIST sleeping in the earth, in the graves, and the tombs shall wake up first. Then those of us who are alive and remain saved shall be caught up together with them in the clouds, to meet the LORD in the air; So we will be with the LORD forever. Therefore encourage one another with these words.

## Trouble and more troubles

When Stephen was stoned to death for being honest, those who stoned him laid down their clothes at a young man's feet, whose name was Saul. Saul continues to breathe threats and slaughter against GOD's disciples until He stopped him head-on. Herod, the king, stretched out his hands and killed James, the brother of John, with the sword. And because he saw that the people were pleased of what he did to James, he took Peter and locked him up. The angel of the LORD appeared and shined a light in the prison and touch Peter on his side. "Up quickly! Put on your sandals. Cast your garment over you and follow me." His chains fell off from his hands.

In the morning, there was commotion among the soldiers as to what had become of Peter. Herod had a thorough search made of the prison but did not find Peter. He examined and ordered that the guards be executed. "But we know that the law is good, if man use it lawfully" (1 Tim. 1:8).

## Herod was struck to death

Herod was very wrathful. He had started a quarrel with the people of Sidon and Tyre. They quickly made allegiance with the king and asked for peace, because they needed help from the king's country. On the day they appointed for the announcement of the supply, Herod, dressed in his royal robe, gave a speech to the people. The people heard the king, and they all gave a loud cry, saying, "This is the voice of a god, not the voice of a man." Because King Herod gave not the glory to GOD, the angel of the LORD struck him down. He was eaten by worms and die.

# Always Give the Glory to God, No Matter What

No matter what political status, financial status, or social status you have achieved, you must make it a point of your duty to give GOD the glory and praise. Don't for one moment think of yourself more than you ought to think. Don't be so flamboyant, believing you have reached your plateau by your own power. Don't be so pugnacious and self-willed, not giving glory and strength to GOD.

> But when you say, I will rise up I will exalt myself and my throne; I will speak eloquently and with power, that all will know for sure who I am. (Luke 14:11)

For whosoever exalteth himself shall be a base; and he that humbles himself shall be exalted. Give unto the LORD ye kindreds of the people; give unto the LORD glory and strength. For great is the LORD, and greatly to be praised: He also is to be feared above all gods. For all the gods of the people are idols, but the LORD made the heavens. (1 Chron. 16:25–28)

Are you aware that GOD has given you a beautiful life? He has given you a marvelous gift. GOD will confront you before you lose the greatest commodity—your life. You have an opportunity. Do not allow your greatest gift to seep away like a slow leak in a tire that is punctured. You are losing pressure all the time, but you are still rolling. You are losing a lot of things you are not even aware. Let's wise up and don't lose anymore. Why should you die before your time? Now is the right time to give back to GOD what He has given unto you.

And I beheld, and I heard a voice of many angels round about the throne and the beast and the elders the number of them was ten thousand times ten thousand, and thousands of thousand, saying with a loud voice, "Worthy is the Lamb that was slain to receive power, and riches, and wisdom, and glory, and blessing." And every creature which is in heaven, and on the earth, and under the earth, and such as are in the sea, and all that are in them, heard me saying, "Blessing and honor, glory, and power, be unto Him that sitteth upon the throne, and unto the Lamb forever and ever." And the four beast said, "Amen." And the twenty-four elders fell down and worship Him that lives for ever and ever.

Change your life. Give the glory to the LORD before your life runs out.

# I AM A WINNER

## Running with an Expectation

I have been young, and I am much older now. When I was a child, running races with my other siblings, I never run to lose. I would always come out to be the winner. There were times when my siblings would win, but not in an honest way. To them, winning comes at any cost, but when we lined up, and the starter said, "Get set, ready, go," the winner was me. When you've to cheat, be dishonest, and unfair in your doings, in your own eyes it seems very good. For the ways of a man is right only in his own eyes.

I turned fifteen years old and was encouraged to join the Boy Scout. I did it. Every week we had to run for one mile and a half on Monday evenings. My friends, for more than two years in the Scout, as much as I can remember, I finished second two times. I was not pleased with finishing second, so I went and worked harder and came out on top. You are a winner; you just don't know it. But now that I have brought this to your attention, you are in the know.

Look at all the little victories you have had in the past? You might have thought because they were so small they were insignificant.

A win is a win. It makes no difference how small it is. When you have conditioned your mind and be positive, you'll see your small winnings in a big way. JESUS told us, "O ye of little faith." If you don't have an expectation to win, don't run. You have to see the winner in you. All the lies they are telling, you are a winner.

I watched a little of the Olympics. I saw the little antics, the jumping up and down, the stretching and the training, all this is building up for the big moment. All of us have a moment or a moment in time. Don't allow this moment to pass you by. Now that you have seen the winner in you, what are you doing about it? Dig deep in your inner self, you will be amazed what you'll find.

As is the natural, so is the spiritual. In the natural, you put in the preparation, time, and hard work, and you will always come out on top a winner. You have to counsel yourself, asking GOD for His help. According to Proverbs 15:22, "Without counsel, plans fail, but with many advisers they succeed." All athletes have trainers to help motivate them. And there is also a trainer in you.

## Run, come, seek the LORD

Right now is time to run for your life. Come and seek the LORD while He may be found. Call Him while He is near. If you tarry, you will be sorry in the end. In this race, it is imperative to "lay aside all the weight and the sin which doth so easily beset us, and let us run with patience the race that is set before us. Looking unto JESUS, the author and finisher of our faith, who for the joy set before Him He endured the cross, scorning its shame, and sat down at the righthand of the throne of GOD." In this race that the Master is calling for you to come while you have time, the reward is not given to those who are fast, swift, or strong. The reward will be given to those who endure to the end.

While you are running, strive not to fall. And if you fall, just ask the Savior to help you, to comfort strengthen and keep you. He is willing to aid you. He will carry you through. The enemy is seeking to devour you. Don't just stay there; GOD cares about you. This troubled wicked world will be destroyed.

Genesis 19:13–24 says, "We will destroy this place, because the outcry to the LORD against its people is so great, that He has sent us to destroy this place." Lot went and spoke to his sons-in-law, who were engaged to marry his daughters. He said to them, "Hurry! Get out of this place, the LORD is about to destroy the city." His son-in-law thought he was joking. While dawn was fast approaching, the angels urged Lot, saying, "Hurry! Take your wife and your two daughters who are here. You will be swept away when the city is destroyed." Lot lingered. The men laid hold on his hand, and upon the hands of his wife, and upon the hand of his two daughters and led them out of the city. The LORD was merciful unto them.

As soon as they had brought them out, one of the angels said, "Flee for your lives! Don't look back, and stop anywhere in the plain! Flee to the mountain, or you will be swept away." But Lot said unto them, "No, my lords, please! Your servant has found favor in your eyes, and you have shown great kindness to me in sparing my life. I can't flee to the mountain, lest some evil come, and I die. Look, here is a town near enough to run to, it is small. Let me flee to it—it is small, isn't it? Then my life will be spared."

The angel said to him, "Very well, I will grant you this request too. I will not overthrow the town you speak of. Flee there quickly. I cannot do anything until you reach there." That is why the town was called Zoar. By the time he reached Zoar, the sun had risen over the land. Then the LORD rained down burning sulfur on Sodom and Gomorrah, from the LORD out of heaven.

## The Lord's Patience Will Come to an End

The LORD's patience came to an end in Noah's day because of the people's hardness of heart, stubbornness, and their wickedness. It grieved the LORD that He had made man. GOD is caring, loving, and long-suffering. The LORD gave men a period of time until Sodom, when He rained down brimstone and fire. The LORD GOD endured in His patience until He brought destruction upon Pharaoh and all the land of Egypt. As the LORD GOD showed His disgust and wrath to the wicked, He delivered the righteous out of all their troubles. Each time the enemy comes, GOD always deliver or make a way for you to escape. With GOD, time is the essence. He has given us enough time to get right and make it right with Him.

> The LORD shall go forth as a mighty man,
> He shall stir up jealousy like a man of war; like
> a warrior he will stir up his zeal; with a shout he
> will raise the battle cry, and will triumph over His
> enemies. For a long time I have kept silent, I have
> been quiet and held myself back. But now, like a

155

woman in childbirth, I cry out, I gasp and pant.
(Isaiah 42:12–14)

The LORD's patience ran short, knowing and seeing all that the enemy was doing to His creation and His heritage. Therefore, GOD said, "For the day of vengeance is in my heart, and the year of my redeemed is come. I looked, and there was no one to help, and I wondered that there was none to give support, so My own arm achieved salvation for Me, and My own wrath sustained Me."

The LORD has given you everything you need to make you happy. Just take a look at all the fun you have had in your time. Look at all pleasures you have delved in. And after you have done everything, eaten everything, you were still in your mess. You were condemned and on your way to hell. So JESUS came that you might have life, and have it in abundance. Now your life will be sweet and your joy is complete. Just put your trust alone in GOD. And don't allow GOD's patience to run out on you. You cannot hide from GOD. He will just come by. That's exactly what JESUS did. While you have a little time, run come and seek the LORD. You will not be sorry you have made this gigantic decision, for the best is yet to come. He is coming as He has promised. Will you be ready? If you were to walk the streets of America and pose this question, "Are you ready?" What do you assume the answer would be?

I am very sure the response would be, "Ready for what?" You have just won the race, are you ready for the medal? Are you ready for your payment? You have just won the Datona, are you ready for the trophy? Are you ready for that paycheck? Now that you have won the race, are you ready to have a good time, pop a bottle of champagne, or go out and celebrate? The answer would be a resounding yes. In the National Football League, one of their famous sayings is, "Are you ready for some football?" It is the question throughout preseason and the regular season.

You have waited this long for the football season to come, will your patience end? I have heard this phrase before, "Heck, yes." Let's get this game started. And let's get it over with, before my patience runs thin. This game will not last forever. It has an end, a period of time. But during the game, you will notice the different factors in the game, some of the players' patience quickly end. They are now, hoping the game will turn out in their favor. These sixteen games will not last. The end is certainly coming. Then you have the playoffs, conference, division, and the Super Bowl. May the best team win.

## Life versus Good and Death versus Evil

I am on the winning team. I have a good owner. He is always looking out for me. He is looking out for all the players who will join His team. You won't have to worry, you don't have to fret. Have you ever noticed your owner's manual? When life and good gets together, it's a winning combination. The result will always be good. The final outcome will be great. "Be strong therefore, and let not your hands be weak: For your work shall be rewarded" (2 Chron. 15:7). Evil has been dominating the game for a long time. For whatever is not good is evil.

"If I do what I do not want to do, I agree that the law of GOD is good. As it is, it's no longer I myself who do it, but it is the sin living in me. For I know that good itself does not dwell in me, that is, in my sinful nature. For I have the desire to do what is good, but I cannot carry it out. I do not do the good I want to do. But the evil I don't want to do is the very thing I find myself doing. If I am doing what I do not want to do, then it's no longer me that does it, but it's the sin living in me that does it. I find the law of sin working in me. What a wretched man I am. But thanks be to GOD, who delivered me through our LORD JESUS CHRIST." "The soul that sin shall die." See, I have set before you this day, life and good, death and evil." Choose life and do good, and you and your family will live. GOD is not unjust to forget your good work.

## Life versus Death

Why don't you just look to JESUS now and live? He came that you might have life, and have it in abundance. "For since we have flesh and blood, GOD too shares in our humanity. That by His death

He might destroy him that had the power of death-that is, the devil. Jesus freed those who all their live were held in slavery by their fear of death" (Heb. 2:14–15). If you live according to the flesh you will die but if you through the Spirit put to death the deeds of your body, you will live (Rom. 8:13).

If at all your body is dead to sin, you are no longer living in it. Sin will not dominate your body or your life. The death that reigned from Adam to Moses, even over those who had not sin as Adam did. To free the people and give them life, the man of GOD, Moses, did as he was instructed. He used the hyssop, dipped it in blood, and sprinkled the people for their cleansing. Moses also applied the blood on the door lintel and on the doorpost. As the angel approached and noticed the blood, he passed the people by. Moses also baptized the people in the cloud and in the sea, in his generation.

Today, if you will believe the form of doctrine that Peter and the other apostles preached, the same as Paul preached, you shall be saved. To be made free from death (sin) and become the servant of righteousness, you must be baptized in water in the name of JESUS CHRIST only, and you shall receive the gift of the Holy Ghost. This is the promise GOD made to those who believe and obey Him. You have now passed from death to life. Keep the faith! Keep your hope alive. For there is no other name given for man to avoid death and be saved but the name JESUS CHRIST.

In order to pass from death to life, you have to do it right. I am not doing this to shame anyone. I am not doing this to persuade or to please anyone. When GOD created you in the womb I was not there. But here I am! Here I write to inform you that my certification is from the Master, JESUS CHRIST. For it pleased GOD to reveal the truth, the whole truth, and nothing but the truth.in me. Here is your chance to have life. I am doing this because I am convinced in whom I've believed. I am sure I have life. You can have it too. Once you have solidified your hold on life, your best is yet to come. Do a self-examination. You will know where you stand. Do you have life, or are you still abiding in death? You have the right to have life. Get up. Stand for life to have it in abundance.

# GET YOUR BUSINESS STRAIGHT

## You Say You Have Time

The urgency of GOD must not be ignored. Get your business straight, for time is winding up. You say you have time. GOD has given a warning against unbelief: "Wherefore as the Holy Ghost says: 'Today, if you hear His voice, harden not your heart.'" When you have heard the truth and after that you know the truth, why linger? In your lingering, you are provoking GOD! You are tempting GOD! I am encouraging you not to allow yourself to be hardened through unbelief. Why would you allow GOD to be aggrieved with you?

All the people that opposed Moses and those who were in unbelief died in the wilderness. You will never make it in life as long as you remain in your wilderness of unbelief. Pick yourself up and shake yourself and come boldly to the throne of GOD's grace, that you may obtain mercy and find help in the time of your need. You may be running out of time. Satan is launching his fiery darts at you, trying to stop your progress. Why don't you let go and let GOD have His way in your life? Your life may be only important to you, but I can assure you that your life is important to GOD.

He will keep on working on you until you admit "I make many mistakes," "I'm a cheater," "I'm a liar," "I'm very deceptive," "I'm unstable," "I know that I was wrong," "I need to get my business straight." Until we allow GOD to step in and give us direction and a purpose, we will never be able to get our business straight.

The best that is yet to come starts here.

JESUS said these words: "All things whatsoever you would that men should do to you, do ye even so to them." This sums up the law and the prophets. Enter in at the straight gate. For wide is the gate and broad is the road that leads to destruction, and many enter through it. But straight is the gate and narrow is the way that leads to life, and only a few find it. You can find the LORD if you really need

Him. He told us who He is. JESUS CHRIST is the way, the truth, and the life. He went away, not to stay. He is the best. He is coming soon.

## The Street That Is Called Straight

In Damascus there was a disciple named Ananias. The LORD called to him in a vision.

"Ananias!"

"Yes, LORD," he answered.

The LORD said unto him, "Go to the house of Judas on Straight Street and ask for a man from Tarsus named Saul, for he is praying. He has seen in a vision, a man named Ananias. Come and place his hands on him to restore his sight."

Brother Ananias was taken back. According to the things he had heard about Saul, "he is a killer. He is a murderer. And he has come here with authority to arrest all who call on your name."

But the LORD said unto Ananias, "Go! This man is my chosen instrument to proclaim my name to the Gentiles and their kings and to the people of Israel. I will show him how much he must suffer for my name."

Ananias came with excitement. He placed his hands on Saul and said, "Brother Saul, the LORD JESUS, who appeared unto thee on road as you were coming here, has sent me so you might receive your sight and be filled with the Holy Ghost." He then baptized Saul in the name of JESUS CHRIST.

Saul went to Straight Street and took care of business. Right away, he went into the temple and testified that JESUS is GOD.

This is the kind of information you will receive when you get to the street called Straight. Then you can run with your new life and tell of the good thing the LORD has done for you. A murderer is now a preacher, turning people from darkness to light, that they might receive forgiveness of sins the inheritance GOD has given among the sanctified. No one can take care of this business for you. I can encourage you, preach to you, and teach you; but you must be willing to get your business straight. You must be obedient to GOD.

You know you have said this many times: "I know that I am a good person. I am trying to help everybody I can. But God knows I'm not perfect." This is just a blatant excuse not to do the right thing. "After you have suffered a while He'll make you perfect. He will establish, strengthen, and settle you" (1 Pet. 5:10).

Saul went to Straight Street and got the understanding that JESUS CHRIST is GOD. When you have this perfect knowledge and the understanding about JESUS, you will be settled in your mind. At Straight Street, you will be informed that JESUS is "Father in creation," "Son in redemption." Today, JESUS is "the Holy Ghost in the church." That's why it is important for you to be baptized in the name JESUS CHRIST. JESUS is the saving name. CHRIST is the anointed one. Come taste and see that the LORD JESUS CHRIST is good.

Do you know Him today? Please don't turn the Savior away. You will fail without Him. Do you know all the amazing things that will change in your life because of Straight Street. It is good to know the LORD. "If you confess your sins He is faithful and just to forgive us of our sins, and cleanse us from all unrighteousness" (1 John 1:9). Because of Saul's obedience, his life changed. If you listen, GOD will do the same thing for you. Do not allow any mountain that is high nor any valley that is low keep you from reaching JESUS.

# HERE HE COMES

## Before God Destroys, He Warned

Just as in Noah's day when the people ignored the warning of the coming flood, they are doing the same thing today. Although they ignored the call to repentance, that did not stop GOD from destroying the people for their evil deeds.

> For the imagination of man's heart is evil from his youth; neither will I again smite the earth, for every living thing as I have done, as long as the earth endures, seedtime and harvest, cold and heat, summer and winter, day and night will never ceased. (Gen. 8:21–22)

Matthew 24:14 says, "And this gospel of the kingdom shall be preached in all the world for a witness unto all nations, and then shall the end come." Before GOD destroys, He warned, "Behold, I have told you before. For as the lightning cometh out of the east, and shineth even unto the west, so shall also the coming of the Son of man be" (Matt. 24:27).

Things calm down for a while. All is well, so it seems. Then there's a breakout. Hell is loose! You have seen wars. You have heard of wars and rumor of wars. You have heard and seen nation rising up against nation. Many lives have been lost in the war in Iraq, at least 4,000. Since the start of the US military operations through April 2021, more than 2,400 American servicemen lost their lives in Afghanistan. Just think about all the lives of civilians and soldiers from these two countries that have been killed.

You have heard and may have seen the recent earthquake in Haiti in which over two thousand lives were lost. Ten years before in that horrific earthquake that took place, more than 310,000 people were killed. Seventeen inches of rain devastated rural Tennessee and about twelve people lost their lives in August 21, 2021. California is currently burning many acres. GOD is showing us what He is about to do. He will bring no more water for destruction but fire this time.

You have read of famine, you have seen famine in different places in the earth, you have heard of pestilences, and you have been in pestilences. How much more can you bear? As it stands right now, many lives have been lost because of COVID-19 and its variants. It has taken the lives of righteous people. It has taken the lives of unrighteous people. These are all or some of the sorrows we face as we march toward the end. GOD has shortened the days, but He has given us enough time to get ourselves ready. But the people have thumbed their nose at the gospel. They have stopped their ears from hearing GOD's word because of their unbelief. We destroy ourselves because we refuse to accept the saving grace of the gospel.

## Where Is the Coming He Promised?

Many are desiring the LORD's return, and the vast many don't believe a word. They follow their evil desires, saying, "Where is the 'coming' He promised?" Ever since our ancestors died, everything had gone on as it had since the beginning of creation. For this, they willingly are ignorant of, long ago. By GOD's word, heaven came into being and the earth was formed out of water and by water; whereby, the world that existed then was overflowed with water, perished. By the same word, the present heavens and earth are reserved for fire, being kept for the day of judgment and destruction of the ungodly.

But do not forget this one thing, dear friends, with the LORD, a day is like a thousand years and a thousand years is like a day. The LORD is not slow in keeping His promise, as some understand slowness. Instead, He is patient with you, not willing that anyone should perish but that all should come to repentance. But the day of the LORD will come as a thief in the night. The heavens will disappear with a great noise; the elements will be destroyed by fire, the earth also; and everything in it shall be burned up. Since everything will be destroyed in this way, what kind of person ought you to be? You ought to live holy and godly lives as you look forward to the day of GOD and speed its coming.

And the elements will melt in the heat. In keeping with His promise, we are looking for a new heaven and a new earth, wherein dwells righteousness. So then, dear friends, since you are looking forward to this day, make every effort to be found blameless, spotless, and be at peace with Him. (2 Pet. 3:4–14 NIV)

## The Unknown Day

But about that day or hour no one knows, not even the angels in heaven, nor the Son, but the Father only. As it was in the days of Noah, so shall it be at the coming of the Son of Man. In the days before the flood, people were eating and drinking, marrying and giving in marriage, until the day Noah entered the ark; they knew nothing about what would happen until the flood came and took them all away. This is how it will be at the coming of the Son of Man. Watch therefore, for you know not what hour your LORD will come.

Who then is the faithful and wise servant, whom the Master has put in charge of the servants in His household to give them the food at the proper time? It will be good for that servant whose Master finds him doing so when He returns. Truly I say unto you, He will make him ruler over all His goods. If that evil servant shall say in his heart, "My Master delays His coming, and he then begins to beat his fellow servants and to eat and drink with drunkards; The Master of that servant will come on a day when he does not expect Him, and at an hour he is not aware of. He will cut him to pieces and assign him a place with the hypocrites, where there will be weeping and gnashing of teeth." (Matt. 24:36–51)

## God has a mansion reserved for you

Song of Solomon 2:10–13 says,

> My Beloved spoke and said unto me, "Arise, my darling, my beautiful one, come with me. The winter is past; The rain is over and gone. Flowers appear on the earth; the season of singing has come, the cooing of doves is heard in our land. The fig tree forms its early fruit; the blossoming vines spread their fragrance. Arise, come, My darling; My beautiful one, come with Me."

When God says something, He says it with eternity in mind. He knows what He is thinking about you exists in eternity. God has a table spread where the saints of God are fed. He invites His chosen to come and dine. "Don't touch this chair, it belongs to my friend. I'm going to bring my friend to sit at the table with me for an encounter."

## A letter

> I wrote this letter to show My love My affection for you. Come close, please! Kiss Me with the kisses of your lips. Your cheeks are comely whom My soul loves. I brought you to My banquet house. Here is My banner I'll be setting over you, My love. You are so lovely. Your mouth is very sweet. You are My friend. My friend, My love, you beautiful angels, know that the love I have for you cost Me My life. Will you return the

favor and love me with your heart, your mind, your soul, and your strength? I created you in My own likeness and breathed the breath of life in you. I know that you messed up yourself along the way, but that's all right. All the things that are wrong, I'll make them right. You have not been honest with yourself. That's a fact. But that's okay! You know that I made you, the boy you are. You know that I made you, the girl you are. You are aware I made you, the man you are. You know I made you, the woman you are. Why are you treating Me as if I've lost My mind? You are aware that I made you and not you yourself. I gave you everything you need according to My riches in glory. I gave you choices because I know your weakness and I know your strength.

I told you that a man should not have sexual relations with another man as you do to a woman. I told you I made you a woman, and he who finds you as his wife finds a good thing and obtains favor from Me. I made you a woman, yet you transgressed My command. Nevertheless! I empathize with you. I've told you your desire shall be to your husband, and he will rule over you.

You hate and hurt others. That's not good. You are hurting yourself. But, oh, how I love you! Now that I have your attention, may I ask you a few more questions? You are aware that the devil hates you, and he wants to destroy you? Do you know he is as a roaring lion, walking about, seeking whom he may devour? If you say, "Lord, You're my refuge and my fortress, my GOD, in You I will trust," I will cover you with My feathers, and under My wings shall you trust. My truth shall be your shield and buckler.

Don't you ever be afraid for the terror by
night, nor the arrow that flies by day, nor the pes-
tilence that walks in darkness, nor the destruction that waste at noonday. One thousand pestilences shall fall at your side and ten thousand at
your right hand, but they will not come near you.
No evil will befall you; neither shall any plague
come near your dwelling. You will tread upon the
lion and adder. The young lion and the dragon
you will trample under your feet. If you set your
love upon Me, I will deliver you. I will set you up
high because you know My name. I will give My
angels charge over you, to keep you in all your
ways. They will bear you up in their hand, lest
you dash your foot against a stone.

Here I am with you, My love. I want you
to have life abundantly. Will you allow My faithful servants to baptize you in the name that I
gave under heaven for men to be saved? Many
have misconstrued My Word because they fail to
understand My speech. I gave My apostles My
Word, and Matthew, the publican, wrote this:
"All power is given unto Me in heaven and in the
earth. Go ye therefore, and teach all nations, baptizing them in the name of the Father, and of the
Son, and of the Holy Ghost: Teaching them to
observe all things whatsoever I have commanded
you. And lo, I am with you always, even unto the
end of the world."

I am GOD! My name is JESUS CHRIST! I
changed not! If you will let My faithful honest
servants baptize you in water, in My name, JESUS
CHRIST, I promise I will fill you with the Holy
Ghost and fire. Your evidence will be speaking
with tongues. Just one more thing! You know
that I love you, right? Don't let anyone deceive

you with their enticing words, not even an angel from heaven. I am giving you this information because I care for you. I hope you enjoy what you've been served, and all the fine things I've told you about My love for you. You may go now! Take good care of yourself and watch out for Me. See you in a little while! Bye!

What manner of man is this who has cost so much controversy? Some called Him Mohammed, some called Him Allah, some called Him Buddha, some called Him Haile Selassie. Thank you, Jesus, for coming down and return to where you were before. You are my GOD. Many people doubt You, but I can't live without You. Thank You, LORD, for your many blessings on me.

## You Can Run but You Can't Hide

Stan, who is sixteen years old, heard a voice, saying, "You need to stop at the nearest holiness church to hear the Word." He had a gun and was on his way to kill a young man or two. That night he stopped by the place of worship. He did not go inside. He stood by the window looking through the windowpanes.

The preacher said, "You, young man standing at the window, I know you have a gun. You are on a mission to kill. Bring me the gun before you are killed."

He said to himself, "I don't know this man. How does he know that I have a gun?"

Another voice spoke to him. "You can't give up the gun. You need to carry out your commission now."

He walked away from the window and proceeded to carry out his mission. When he got to the location where he was to take the lives of the people, the first voice spoke to him again.

"I am giving you one more chance to change your ways."

There was another holiness church nearby. While he was passing, the voice said to him, "Go and hear the Word of GOD."

He went, but he stood outside the window, looking through the windowpanes.

The preacher looked at him and said, "You, young man standing at the window, bring me the gun. Come to the Lord before you lose your life."

This time he was obedient. He went and gave the weapon up. He was baptized in the name of Jesus Christ that same night, and the Lord filled him with the Holy Ghost and power, and he spoke in tongues. The devil thought he had him. The Lord gave him a chance to make it right. He accepted the call, and today he is the pastor of that church.

# BEHOLD, I COME QUICKLY AND MY REWARD IS WITH ME

## The New Heaven and the New Earth

I saw a new heaven and earth for the first heaven and earth were passed away, along with the sea. I John saw the holy city, the new Jerusalem, coming down from God out of heaven, prepared as a bride adorned for her husband. I heard a great voice out heaven saying, "Behold, the tabernacle of God is with men, He will dwell with them, they shall be His people. God Himself shall be with them, and be their God. He shall wipe away all tears from their eyes. There shall be no more death, sorrow, crying, pain, for the former things are passed away. He that overcometh shall inherit all things. I will be his God, and he shall be My son.

But the fearful, unbelieving, abominable, murderers, whoremongers, sorcerers, idolaters, and all liars, shall have their part in the lake which burneth with fire and brimstone, which is the second death." He carried me away in the spirit to a great mountain and shewed me the great city, the holy Jerusalem, descending out of heaven from God. The city lies foursquare. The length, and breath, and height of the city are equal. The city has twelve gates made with pearls. The street of the city is pure gold as transparent glass. The city has no temple. The Lord God Almighty and the Lamb are the temple of the city. The glory of God is the light of the city.

177

The nation of them that are saved shall walk in the light of it. The kings of the earth do bring their glory and honor into it. The city will be open all day. There shall in no wise enter into it anything that defiles, neither whosoever works abomination, or makes a lie, but they which are written in the Lamb's book of life. (Rev. 21)

## The Book of life and the Books of sin and death

And I saw the dead, small and great, stand before GOD. The books were opened, and another book was opened, which is the book of life. The dead were judged out of those things which were written in the books, according to their works. The sea gave up the dead which were in it; and death and hell delivered up the dead which were in them. They were judged every man according to their works. Death and hell were cast into the lake of fire; this is the second death. Whosoever was not found written in the book of life was cast into the lake of fire. (Rev. 20:12–15)

When you turn to GOD from your sins, He writes your name in the Book of Life because of your obedience. There are many books for the disobedient, heathen, sinners, and the wicked to have their sentence read to them and of all their ungodly acts they have committed in their ungodliness.

## Let Us Worship God

Let us sing unto the LORD with thanksgiving, for He alone is excellent. Let us give Him praise in glory. Let us praise Him with dancing. When we send the praises up, He sends the blessings down. Let us never cease to praise the LORD, for He has done great things for us. Let us praise the Savior all the day long.

## The Time Is at Hand

Let him that hear the Word, come. Let him that is thirsty, come. Whosoever will, let him take of the water of life freely. JESUS is coming with a shout of acclamation to take us home. This should be joy to your soul. The vilest offender who truly believes that very moment from JESUS, a pardon you will receive. He will make your trusting heart His home. He will turn your sadness to gladness. He will give you perfect peace and rest. Cheer up, my friend! Death will come to take you home, but only to sleep. Death will come to take your love ones away. It may be hard to understand why. Revelations 14:13 says,

> And I heard a voice from heaven saying unto me, "Write, blessed are the dead which die in the LORD from henceforth." "Yes," says the Spirit, they will rest from their labor, for their deeds do follow them.

## Your Right to the Tree of Life

Genesis 3:22–24 says,

> And the LORD GOD said, "Behold, the man is become as one of Us, to know good and evil: and now, lest he put forth his hand, and take also of the tree of life, to eat, and live forever."

Therefore, the LORD sent him forth from the garden of Eden to till the ground from whence he was taken. So He drove the man out, and He placed at the east of the garden of Eden cherubim and a flaming sword that turned every way, to keep the way of the tree of life.

> For the Word of GOD is quick and active. Sharper than any two-edged sword, it penetrates even to dividing soul and spirit, joints and marrow; It judges the thoughts and the attitudes of

the heart. Nothing in all creation is hidden from GOD's sight. Everything is uncovered and laid bare before the eyes of Him to whom we must give account. (Heb. 4:12)

Blessed are they that do His commandments, that they may have a right to the tree of life, and may enter in through, the gates into the city. For outside are dogs, those who practice magic arts, whoremongers, murderers, the idolaters, and whosoever loves and makes a lie. He that is unjust, let him be unjust still. He that if filthy let him be filthy still. He that is righteous, let him be righteous still; and he that is holy, let him be holy still. (Rev. 22:11–15)

## Sitting Down with Abraham, and Isaac, and Jacob in Heaven

Then JESUS went through the towns and the villages, teaching as He made His way to Jerusalem. Someone asked Him, "LORD, are only a few people going to be saved?"

Jesus answered, "You, make every effort to enter through the narrow door because many, I tell you, will try to enter and will not be able to. Once the owner of the house gets up and closes the… door, you will stand outside knocking and pleading, 'Sir, please open the door for us.' But He will answer, 'I don't know you or where you come from.' Then you will say, 'We ate and drank with you, and you taught in our streets.' But He will reply, 'I don't know you or where you come from. Get away from Me, all you evildoers!' There will be weeping there and gnashing of teeth when you see Abraham, Isaac, Jacob, and all the prophets in the kingdom of GOD. But you yourselves thrown out. People will come from the east and west, and north and south, and will take their places at the feast in the kingdom of GOD."

Can you hear the voice of JESUS sweetly calling, "Will you come and work for Me today? Will you bring to me the lost and those who are dying? Will you point them to the narrow way? Many are dying in their shame and their sin. Just listen to their sad, bitter cry. Hurry, brother, hurry to the rescue. Do not let this moment pass you by."

The LORD wrestles with you until you face the facts. You need to enter through the straight gate to do His will. GOD wrestles with you for you to realize you are wasting your time. JESUS said, "Seek ye first the kingdom of GOD" (Matt. 6:33).

# MY FLIGHT TO HEAVEN, THE NEW JERUSALEM

## My Visit to the New Home of My Soul

"The time to be happy is now, and the place to be happy is here. The way to be happy, to make others happy, is to have a little heaven down here." This is a song they used to sing in praise service since 1968 up until now. When you receive the Holy Ghost, it is the kingdom of GOD in you. It is just a taste of heaven.

It was February 1989. In a vision, a man came to me in shining raiment. He gave my new body a space suit, greenish in color. He said, "It's time to leave, put this on."

So I put on my new body and was caught up into the clouds of heaven. Although it seems as if I was alone on this journey, my gliding into the heavens was spectacular. It was a long flight.

On reaching the city, a voice said to me, "You have reached your destination."

When I landed, I approached the first gate. It was shut closed. I could see Peter through the transparent glass bars. I cried with a loud voice, "Peter, Peter, Peter, let me in."

He responded, "Who do you need?"

"I need to see JESUS, my LORD," I said.

He came and opened the gate and let me in and said unto me, "This is your home. You are free! You can go anywhere you desire."

The walls of the city were like marble. The pavement and the street were shiny and white as snow. The humongous city was a sight to behold and was lit by the glory of GOD. As I did my walkabout the city, I was singing to myself this song, "This place is beautiful this place is beautiful, this place is beautiful, it's the home of the free. I need to see JESUS! Need to see JESUS, I need to see JESUS, my Savior and King."

Suddenly JESUS appeared, shining as the sun and His eyes as balls of fire.

I cried with a lamentable voice and said, "My GOD! My GOD! My GOD! What a beautiful place."

I awoke from my sleep, still giving GOD the praise, saying, "My GOD! My GOD! My GOD! What a beautiful place."

As you face the storms of life, with all the bitterness, misery, and strife, just ask the LORD to lay His mighty hands on you. He will raise you up, with your mind set on the things above, where JESUS, the CHRIST, is sitting on the right hand of power. For if you are dead, your life must be hid in CHRIST in GOD. "When CHRIST who is our life shall appear, then shall we also appear with Him in glory" (Col. 3:4).

If you have not yet started the mission, today is your day to start. Get on the glory road. JESUS is soon to come, and heaven is in view. At times this road gets rough, but JESUS will carry you and see you through. Little by little pull yourself away from the things that are holding you captive. Why don't you let go and let GOD have His way, for the best is yet to come.

## Why Have You Waited So Long?

Why are you waiting, brother? Why are you waiting, my sister? JESUS is standing at the door of your heart. He is waiting for you to let Him in. He sees the many tears you cried running down your face. He wants to wipe them away. He has seen all the rainbows you have reached for, but only in vain. He knows the man behind the curtain who is making things very appealing, only to hold you back.

Satan desires to use you for his own purpose, to ruin your life in the end. He was cast out of heaven for his rebellion. Now he is causing you to rebel on GOD. That's the reason you must walk closely to JESUS's side. Cling to Him, so that visit to heaven you are waiting for will come at last. You must realize who it is that is motivating you. The Holy Spirit desires to use you. Why are you waiting so long?

# THE END

# The End

If we keep thinking about the end, we will be more effective and stronger as people of GOD. It keeps us focused on our goal. The end should remind us that GOD is working on us, and all things will be accomplished in His perfect timing. Have you been meditating or thinking on the way the world will end? You can't talk about the end without talking about JESUS. Our salvation has already been purchased by JESUS CHRIST and secured at the cross. He was taken down from the cross and placed in a tomb (grave). Then after three days and three nights, JESUS arose.

He remained here for over forty days, reassuring the disciples of His promise. Whatever will happen in the future, our hope is secured in the reality that JESUS acted decisively in history and restored our hope of a broken relationship with GOD. You can now honestly say, "GOD, I am convinced and I am sure that You are my Father, and there is no doubt about it."

Because of what our GOD did on our behalf, history is moving us toward a glorious end. History changed when JESUS came to earth, born, died, and rose again and ascended to heaven. Everything will be changed again when He returns. The righteous dead will awake and be given their new body. The righteous ones still living, looking, longing, and waiting for JESUS's return will be changed to their new body and be caught up with those from the dead to be with the LORD in the air.

Just as the judge revoked my supervised release and discharged the petitions and violations dated February 6, 2020; so will the earth, the grave, hell, and the sea relinquish those who are held captive. And this one thing you can be assured of, that He who began a good work in you will continue His good work until it is finally finished, on the day when JESUS CHRIST returns. For He is the best and is yet to come. He will not tarry.

The wicked in his pride does persecute the poor. The wicked make their boast of their heart's desire. They blessed the covetous and the wicked whom GOD hates. Through arrogance and pride, the wicked changed their countenance and will have nothing to do with my GOD and are not thinking about Him. The wicked said, "Who is looking? Who will know about my deceit and my fraud? Who will see me sitting in my lurking places, city, state, town, and the villages?" The LORD will not allow the wicked to prevail. He will judge them with the power of His word.

Psalm 9:17 says, "The wicked shall be turned into hell, and all the nations that forget GOD. Where their worms that eats them do not die, and the fire is not quenched."

And I saw an angel come down from heaven, having the key of the bottomless pit and a great chain in his hand. And he laid hold on the dragon, that old serpent, which is the Devil, and Satan, and bound him a thousand years, and cast him into the bottomless pit, and shut him up and set a seal upon him, that he should deceive the nations no more, until the thousand years be fulfilled and after that he must be loosed a little season.

I saw thrones, on which were seated those who had been given authority to judge And I saw the souls of those who had been beheaded because of their testimony about JESUS and because of the Word of GOD. They had not worshipped the beast, or his image, and had not received his mark on their foreheads, or in their hands. They came to life and reigned with CHRIST a thousand years.

(The rest of the dead did not come to life until the thousand years were ended.) When the thousand years are over, Satan will be released from his prison, and will go out to deceive the nations in the four corners of the earth—Gog and Magog—and to gather them for the battle. In number, they are like the sand of the sea shore. They marched across the breadth of the earth and surrounded the camp of GOD's people, and the city He loves. But fire came down from heaven and devoured them.

And the devil, that deceived them, was thrown into the lake of burning sulfur, where the beast, and the false prophet had been thrown. They will be tormented day and night for ever and ever. (Rev. 1:10)

May the GOD of peace who shed His blood and gave us a new covenant and a promise equip you with everything good for doing His will. May the LORD work in you what is pleasing in His sight, for the best is yet to come. Come, LORD JESUS, come! You are the best.

# ABOUT THE AUTHOR

Julius Williams was brought up in the Shiloh Apostolic Church in Manchester, Jamaica. He developed a love for the Lord and accepted Him as his personal savior. He was baptized in water in the name of Jesus Christ and received the Holy Spirit with the evidence of speaking with other tongues as the Spirit gives utterance. The word of God is dwelling in him richly. He hopes that all men will come to the knowledge that there is only one God, who came into the world as Jesus Christ, to save us from our sins. He knows that the son of God has come and has given us an understanding that we may know Him, that is true. He is in Him, that is true, even in the Son, Jesus Christ. This is the true God and eternal life. Julius Williams is not afraid to let *The Best Is Yet to Come* be known, to make the vision plain as he shares his thoughts of some of the things that God has shown him. He has been encouraging, preaching, and teaching the word of God constantly to all who will listen. The word of God has made him wise unto salvation.